By Carol Barkin and Elizabeth James

Slapdash Sewing
Slapdash Cooking
Slapdash Alterations
Slapdash Decorating

By Elizabeth James and Carol Barkin

The Simple Facts of Simple Machines

Slapdash Decorating

Slapdash Decorating

**Carol Barkin
and Elizabeth James**

Illustrated by Rita Flodén Leydon

Lothrop, Lee & Shepard Company • New York
A Division of William Morrow & Co., Inc.

Copyright © 1977 by Carol Barkin and Elizabeth James
All rights reserved. No part of this book may be reproduced or utilized in any form or by any means, electronic or mechanical, including photocopying, recording or by any information storage and retrieval system, without permission in writing from the Publisher. Inquiries should be addressed to Lothrop, Lee & Shepard Company, 105 Madison Ave., New York, N. Y. 10016. Printed in the United States of America.

1 2 3 4 5 6 7 8 9 10

Library of Congress Cataloging in Publication Data
Barkin, Carol.
   Slapdash decorating.
   SUMMARY: Quick, easy, and inexpensive ways to create or improvise with furniture, windows, walls, floors, and accessories to give your room a new look.
   1. Interior decoration—juvenile literature.
2. Handicrafts—juvenile literature. [1. Interior decoration. 2. Handicraft] I. James, Elizabeth, joint author. II. Leydon, Rita Flodén. III. Title.
NK2115.B28   747'.77   77-22241
ISBN 0-688-41813-9
ISBN 0-688-51813-3 lib. bdg.

Contents

The Slapdash Method   12

Decorating Decisions   13
    Making a Plan • The Over-all Look •
    Tools and Materials • Creative Scavenging

Furniture   23
    Fixing Up Old Furniture • *Slapdash Tip: See-through Safety* • *Slapdash Tip: A Neat Trick for Knobs* • *Slapdash Tip: Slap Together a Slipcover!* • Fixing an Uncomfortable Bed • *Slapdash Tip: Hide an Extra Bed!* • Using Unfinished Furniture • Making Your Own Furniture • Board and Cinder-block Bookcase • *Slapdash Tip: Step Right Up!* • Desk • Vanity Dresser • *Slapdash Tip: Mirror, Mirror on the Wall* • Vanity Stool • *Slapdash Tip: Comfort Counts!* • Night Table

Closets and Storage Space   43
    Organizing Your Closet • *Slapdash Tip: A Loopy Idea* • *Slapdash Tip: Handy Hang Ups* • Building a Storage Unit • *Slapdash Tip: Show Off Something Special!* • *Slapdash Tip: Create a Corner Cupboard!* • Making a Storage Chest/Window Seat

Windows   53
    Slapdash Tip: Make a Window Display! • *Slapdash Tip: Mirror Magic* • Decorating Ready-made Shades • *Slapdash Tip: Choose Your Own View!* • Making Your Own Shades • Shirred Curtains • *Slapdash Tip: Preserve Your Privacy!* • Café Curtains • Full-length Curtains or Drapes • "Fake" Curtains or Drapes •

Slapdash Tip: Make Your Window More Important! • Tiebacks • Valances • Decorative Shower Curtain

Bed Coverings 71
Transforming an Old Bedspread • Super Easy Bedspread • *Slapdash Tip: Spread Some Paint Around!* • Making a Bedspread • Comforter • Matching Dust Ruffle • *Slapdash Tip: If You Don't Have Box Springs* • Quilted Bedspread

Floors 85
Jazzing Up a Room-size Rug • Safari Rug • Patchwork Area Rug • Floor Pillows • *Slapdash Tip: Soften Up Your Study Chair!*

Walls 93
Hangings • Illusion Bed Canopy • *Slapdash Tip: For That Romantic Look* • Posters • Do-it-yourself "Wallpaper" • Framing Pictures • Hanging Pictures • Bulletin Board • *Slapdash Tip: Glitter Glamour* • *Slapdash Tip: Make a Ribbon Display!* • Wall Headboard

Accessories 104
Fixing Up Old Lamps and Lampshades • *Slapdash Tip: Light a Matching Lamp!* • Making a Lamp • Containers • Wastebaskets • *Slapdash Tip: How About a Hamper?* • Desk-top Accessories • Vanity-top Accessories • Dresser Accessories • Drawer Organizers • Plants and Living Things • *Slapdash Tip: Two Points for Plants!* • *Slapdash Tip: A Living Window Frame*

Index 123

The Slapdash Method

Do you sometimes walk into your room and say, "I can't stand the way this place looks!" Don't you wish there were some quick and easy way to give your room a super new look? In this book you will find ideas for fixing up your whole room. Even a few changes can make your room a more comfortable and inviting place to live in.

Slapdash decorating doesn't require any complicated procedures or technical know-how. You don't have to be a master carpenter or worry about a lot of picky details. You'll discover ingenious ways of making the most of what you already have. Best of all, "slapdash" means you won't have to invest a lot of time or money.

The measurements in this book are given in inches and feet and in *approximate* metric equivalents. Some products are now sold in metric sizes while others, like fabric and lumber, are still measured in inches and feet. Use the numbers as a rough guide—your own ideas and space will determine your exact needs.

You can follow the suggestions given for each project or you can modify them in your own way to make your room reflect the real you. Feel free to experiment and to add your own creative touches. You'll be amazed at how easy it is to give your room a new personality the slapdash way!

Decorating Decisions

Before you get out the paintbrush and scissors, give a little thought to how you use your room. Is it a place where you study as well as sleep? Do you and your friends lounge around in your room after school? Do you share a room with your sister or brother? Maybe you need more space for your hobby equipment. Or you might have a collection of models or seashells you'd like to display.

MAKING A PLAN
The next step is to decide how to arrange your furniture to make the best use of the space you have. Start with the big pieces because they take up the most room. If you need new pieces of furniture, don't forget to include them in your plan.

If you share a room, you may want to put in a room divider. Even if it doesn't go all the way to the ceiling, it gives a feeling of two separate areas. Decide where to put the divider but make sure that the division of the space is fair. (It's not fair for one person to have all the windows!)

Some good room dividers are a storage unit (see page 46) or a board and cinder-block bookcase (see page 32). If you can find an old folding screen, you could refinish it with paint and contact paper. Or try stapling attractive fabric (such as printed sheets) to one side and pasting a poster collage to the other side. Anything that isn't too bulky and has two nice-looking sides makes a fine room divider. If you have a bookcase with a back on it, why not nail Celotex or glue cork squares on the back for a bulletin board?

Even if you have your own room, you may want a study area and a sleeping area. These don't need to be separated by a divider, although you can use one if you have the space. Just make sure you don't end up with a room that's cut up into so many little areas that there's no space to walk around.

When you decide where you want your bed or your desk, keep the wall area in mind as well as the floor space. If your window is a little drafty it might not be a good idea to put your bed right under it. If you put your bed in a corner it will be easy to lounge on but harder to make. You may like the idea of sitting at your desk and looking out the window. But maybe you would rather have your desk up against a wall so you can hang a bulletin board over it. These are all options to be considered.

It's fun to make a floor plan of your room. This way you can try out new arrangements on paper first. You can draw your plan freehand to get a rough idea. But for a small room you may want to be more exact so you can see whether everything will fit before you start moving furniture. Measure your room and then draw an outline of its shape on regular graph paper; allow 1 square of paper for 1 square foot (¼ square meter). Be sure to put in all doors and windows and any other permanent objects like radiators. Then measure the length and width of each piece of furniture; cut out pieces of graph paper or cardboard to correspond with these shapes. Now you can label these pieces and move them around on the floor plan outline until you find an arrangement that works. Just keep in mind that these pieces don't show the height of your furniture. You'll have to visualize how the various pieces will look standing next to one another; for instance, a whole wall of tall pieces could make your room look very unbalanced.

Don't forget to mark your floor plan to show how far the doors open into the room so they won't bump into your furniture. Also, remember not to block your windows with furniture that is too tall and to leave space in front of any furniture that has drawers so you can open them. And of course you won't

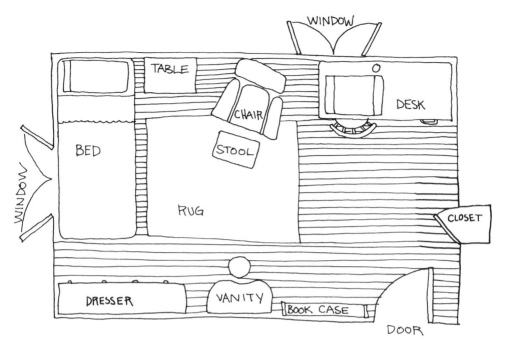

want to put solid pieces of furniture in front of heat registers or radiators.

THE OVER-ALL LOOK

Now you can decide on the over-all look or feeling you want your room to have. You might like American Indian colors and motifs. Do you prefer a dark, woodsy feel or a fresh floral look? Maybe your heart's desire is a pastel room full of frills and ruffles. Or perhaps you like the clean, modern look of simple designs and bold colors. Another possibility is to design your room around your favorite sport. Just remember that whatever you choose is what you'll be looking at for quite a while.

Color and texture are two key considerations in creating a look for your room. Dark colors tend to make your room look smaller, and of course darker. On the other hand, dark colors used sparingly can provide a dramatic look. Light colors reflect more light, making your room seem larger and brighter. Pastels are restful to look at, but a room of nothing but pastels may be too bland. Strong colors make good accents but too much strong color makes it difficult to relax in your room. Try using the colors that appeal to you; you may come up with unique color combinations that look fantastic. But don't use so many different colors that your room looks like a hodgepodge.

Often you can use two basic colors and a third as an accent so your room looks put together without being boring. Earth tones like oranges, browns, and golds with dark green accents are warm and soothing; just be careful it doesn't all look too dark. For a room that doesn't get much light you might want to use spring flower colors like clear yellow and white with clean oranges, reds, or blues as accents. A room with beachy colors like pale beige and blues can be given some zing with rich maroon. Of course, if your room is carpeted in royal blue or you have a beautiful green bedspread that you want to keep, you'll need to use this color as a starting point in choosing the other colors for your room.

Prints and patterns can also be combined. Flower prints can look great with stripes, and polka dots might combine well with checks. Use some caution, though, or you may end up with a room that looks too busy.

The textures you choose give another dimension to your decorating scheme. It's rather uninteresting to use the same texture everywhere. You might use smooth and rough textures in the same color. Or add rough-textured accents to a smooth-surfaced room.

As you choose fabrics and coverings for walls and furniture, look for materials that are washable and easy to care for. You'll want sturdy fabric on your bed if you and your friends often flop there with your shoes on. And if you do messy hobby projects you'll want a surface that's easy to wipe off.

It's easy to make a variety of window, bed, and floor coverings that will give your room a put-together look. You can express yourself in colors, patterns, and textures. Look for fabrics that go well together. You can use the same fabric for your drapes and bedspread, but then you'll probably want to use a contrasting fabric for pillows or a small rug. Experiment with interesting combinations, but don't forget you'll be spending a lot of time in this room; be sure that what you choose is something you can live with for more than two weeks.

When you start looking around for fabric, don't neglect the bedding section of department or discount stores. Sheets are ideal for many purposes because they come in such large sizes and are already hemmed or finished at the edges. Of course, they are washable. And they're available in a huge variety of colors and patterns. Watch for sales—you might find just what you want at a lower price. You can also check stores that specialize in upholstery and drapery fabrics. These fabrics are handy because they come in very wide widths, but they are often expensive and must be dry-cleaned.

You don't have to choose all your colors and fabrics right away, so long as you have a general idea of the look you want. Just get the big things taken care of. Then keep your eyes open and maybe you'll find exactly the right accent to spark your decorating scheme.

TOOLS AND MATERIALS

Most of the tools you will need are probably available around the house. Anything you don't have you can buy as you need it

from a hardware or discount building supply store. Here are the basic tools you will need:

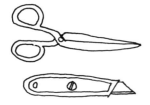

Measuring equipment—a yardstick, tape measure, and ruler will all be useful;

Cutting equipment—kitchen shears for cutting paper, sewing scissors for cutting fabric, and a utility knife for cutting heavy cardboard and carpeting;

Sewing equipment—medium-sized needle and/or a sewing machine, assorted threads, straight pins, a couple of safety pins;

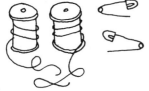

Adhesives—white glue, rubber cement, masking tape;

Hardware—stapler, thumbtacks, pushpins, cup hooks, upholstery tacks, molly bolts, and nails (assorted sizes);

Home repair equipment—hammer, pliers, screwdriver;

Handy optional equipment—pinking shears and a staple gun.

When choosing the materials for your room, get the fabrics and contact paper you want first and then get your paints. Paint can be mixed to any color you want, so it's much easier to match the paint to the fabric than the other way around.

For fabrics, look in large fabric stores or the yard goods section of a big department store. If you can find a discount fabric store you'll have just as large a selection at lower prices. Be sure you're happy with your choices before the salesperson starts cutting. Once cut, fabrics cannot be returned. The salesperson can probably help you figure out how much material you need for your project and can tell you whether the fabric is washable and sturdy enough for your purpose. Sometimes you can buy remnants of fabric at a fraction of the original cost. And, of course, don't forget to look in the sheet section before you buy regular yard goods.

Hardware stores, five-and-tens, discount stores, and building supply stores are good sources for most of the other things you'll need to decorate your room. If you're using contact paper, check around to see who has the widest selection. When you go to buy paint, be sure to take a swatch of your fabric with you so you can choose a color that goes well with it. And tell the salesperson what you are planning to do. There are so many different kinds of paint that it is often hard to tell which kind you want. Your salesperson will also be able to help you choose the right kind and size of brush. You don't need an expensive one, but a really cheap one will leave more brush marks on your painted surface. In fact, be sure to ask salespeople for advice wherever you buy decorating supplies. They are usually helpful and knowledgeable and can sometimes give you tips on new products that can make your project even easier and faster.

When you begin work on a decorating project, gather up all the things you'll need so they will be handily available. And use common sense about protecting the area you're working in. If possible, painting should be done outdoors on lots of newspaper. And use newspaper *behind* what you're spray-painting as well as under it. If you are painting something with drawers, take the drawers out and paint them separately. Otherwise, you're very likely to paint them shut!

If you have to paint indoors, do it in a well-ventilated room as paint fumes can make you feel quite sick. Move everything else away from the object you are going to paint and cover the entire surrounding area with plenty of newspaper. Be careful not to walk or sit in smears of wet paint on the paper or you'll track it all over the house. If an accident does happen, stop and clean it up immediately. You'll have a much better chance of getting the stain out.

When you are cutting things with a utility knife, be sure to cut on lots of layers of newspaper or cardboard. And treat the knife with respect; it can easily slice your finger to the bone!

CREATIVE SCAVENGING

Before you buy anything, scrounge around the house. You may find something that's just what you need. And check with neighbors and friends to see if they're getting rid of any useful junk.

Look at things creatively! A mug without a handle or an old chipped teapot might be a perfect container for pencils, combs, or dried flowers. An old mirror may need only a refurbished frame to look terrific over your dresser. And a beat-up foot locker can become a comfortable seat under a window or at the foot of your bed. You might even find a crummy old kitchen chair that would make a fine desk chair with just a coat of new paint (tighten any loose joints with white glue before painting). A discarded end table or coffee table might be just right as a bedside stand; if it's really ugly, cover it with a cloth that goes with your room.

While you're scavenging for these hidden treasures, take a look at model rooms and display areas in furniture and department stores. Although these are meant to show off expensive new furnishings, you might pick up some great ideas that could be adapted quite inexpensively. You might see a cushion made from an Oriental rug. If there is a worn-out rug in your house, you could use it to make a sturdy and beautiful floor pillow (be sure to ask first). Or you just might see an unusual combination of colors that appeals to you.

Local craft fairs can be a source of terrific new ideas for accessories. Examples of sand painting or new ways of decorating with beads, shells, or found objects might inspire you to use these techniques in your own way.

Keep your eyes open for new ideas everywhere. Even if you don't like all the details of something you see, it might give you the key to a decorating problem that has stumped you. And if you see something great that looks complicated and expensive, maybe you can figure out a way to get the same effect slapdash!

Furniture

Furniture is the first thing to think about in decorating a room. Because it is bulky and takes up floor space, you have to plan the rest of the room around it. Even more important, the kind of furniture that's in a room determines how the room can be used. It's hard to sleep in a bedroom without a bed! And if you need to use the room to study, you'll want someplace to read and write.

If your room is crammed with so much furniture that you can hardly move around, the first step will be to get rid of the least useful pieces. Then think about what you'd ideally like to have in your room. For a room that's to be both a bedroom and a place to study you'll probably want:

        a bed
        a chest of drawers
        a desk and a desk chair
        a night table
        a lamp or two.

Depending on how much space you have, you might want:

        a bookcase
        a comfortable chair for reading
        another bed for overnight guests.

Now take a look at the furniture you already have. Don't worry too much about how it looks; most of that can be fixed. Check each piece to see if it functions properly. Is the desk you have large enough for your present needs? Is your bed comfortable and firm enough? If you have a desk chair, is it sturdy rather than wobbly?

Once you know what you need, start scrounging. Check the attic and the basement. Ask your relatives and neighbors whether they have any furniture they're getting rid of. Look in Salvation Army stores and thrift shops for furniture bargains.

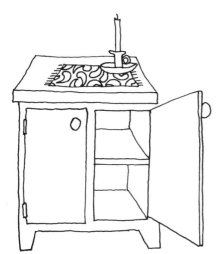

Wood furniture is expensive even secondhand, though, so make sure you can use what you buy.

Keep an open mind about the old pieces you find. An old telephone stand or a sewing stand could make a useful and unique night table. Or how about a low nursery table that all your brothers and sisters have outgrown? A beat-up kitchen table might be just the right size for a new desk. Then you could put cardboard filing boxes or a low bookcase under one end for your papers and supplies. Even an old-fashioned and scarred dresser can look great when you finish repainting it or covering it with contact paper.

And be sure to look for double-duty items. A small chest of drawers could make a terrific nightstand and also hold jewelry and sewing supplies or school papers. A little cupboard is more useful than a small table because you can store stuff inside. Since adequate storage space will probably be one of your biggest problems, anything you can put stuff *in,* as well as on top of, is another step in solving this dilemma.

FIXING UP OLD FURNITURE

The salesperson at your local hardware, paint, or discount building supply center can be the best source of advice on refinishing furniture. But be sure you let this person know that you want to do something quick and easy. Almost any surface can be painted without stripping off the old finish. Just be sure the original surface is clean and dry before you start to paint. Household detergent will take off all that old grime and furniture wax.

Water-soluble or latex paint is great because you can wash the paint off your hands and the brushes, while it's still wet. Enamel or oil-base paint is hard to clean off, even with turpentine, but it gives a hard, shiny finish and is the traditional choice for painting wood furniture. Both kinds of paint come in any color you could possibly want, so you can make your furniture blend right into whatever color scheme you've chosen. And of course spray paint might be a good choice for small pieces.

A word of warning: you might think it would be nice to refinish your furniture in a natural wood stain. But this requires stripping off the old finish first—a difficult, time-consuming, and messy job. If you are determined to try it, work on one drawer first to see whether you really want to spend the time and energy needed for the whole job.

Another solution for covering old finishes is contact paper. It comes in a wide variety of colors and patterns, including wood-grain patterns. It requires a little patience to put it on smoothly, but once it's on it stays. Be sure to clean your furniture first. You could try combining paint and contact paper on various pieces for an interesting effect. Contact paper is especially good for flat surfaces that get a lot of use, like desk and dresser tops, because it can be cleaned with soap and water over and over.

☆ slapdash tip
See-through Safety

Here's a way to protect a painted or varnished wood surface from water rings and pencil marks: cover it with transparent contact paper! This gives a tough, waterproof finish that can take lots of abuse and still lets the original surface show through. Try it on windowsills where you water your plants, too!

Secondhand furniture may often be missing a few knobs and handles. Or you might not like the ones that are there. Some of these are rather expensive to buy new, but you'll probably be able to find something you like that you can afford. Look in a hardware or building supply store. New hardware can give an old chest of drawers a completely different look. If you get plain wooden knobs, you can paint them to match or contrast with the rest of the piece of furniture.

☆ slapdash tip
A Neat Trick for Knobs

To paint wooden knobs, remove them from the drawers. Twist the original screw or a longer one into each knob. Then, using the screw as a handle, dip each knob into the paint. Stand the screw end in the corrugated edge of a cardboard box until the paint dries. No mess—no brush marks!

Here are some examples of what you can do with a weird collection of ratty old furniture. How about painting each drawer of that hideous dresser a different color? You could start with pale pink on the top drawer and use darker shades for each of the other drawers until you end up with maroon at the bottom. Then use a zingy striped sheet of matching contact paper for the top and paint the sides the color of the middle or top drawer.

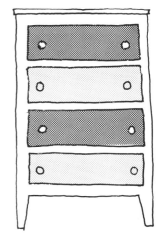

Did you find an old end table or magazine rack that used to be in the living room but was finally shoved into the basement because the veneer was all chipped? Of course one solution is to paint it. But what about covering the top with a collage of postcards or those beautiful old calendar pictures you've been saving just because you like them? Any "scrapbook" items can be used for a collage as long as they are flat. Just glue them on and cover the surface with plastic or with polyurethane spray.

It's very expensive to reupholster an overstuffed chair, but you can give a grungy one a new look by using a "throw." You need something fairly heavy, like an old bedspread or drape, a moth-eaten afghan, or a colorful but holey blanket. As long as it's big enough, you can tuck your throw down deep all around the chair cushion and drape it over the back, sides,

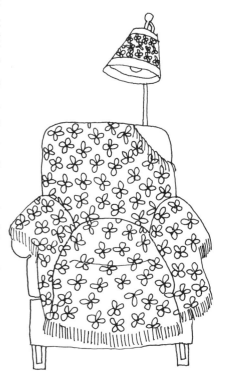

and front so that none of the stains or holes show.

Slap Together a Slipcover!

One of the latest looks in slipcovers is a baggy, loose-fitting cover pulled together with a drawstring at the bottom—kind of like harem trousers for furniture! If your throw is large enough, make a hem all around the edges. Then run a tape or cord through this hem. Pull it tight around the furniture legs and tie.

You could cover a chair cushion or the seat of a stool the same way—make two or three to give your room an instant personality change!

A BRIGHT SLIPCOVER FOR A STOOL

Have you discovered one of those old metal kitchen cabinets sitting around somewhere? It may be ugly, but it can be very useful for storing things—a tall one might be just right for keeping papers or hobby supplies neatly organized; a short one could work as a nightstand or for one of the supports of your desk (see page 34). Transform this monstrosity with spray paint made especially for metal. Or how about gluing fabric on the sides and felt or felt contact paper on the top?

FIXING AN UNCOMFORTABLE BED

An uncomfortable bed can turn you into a real grouch! But a new bed is a very expensive purchase. So here are some tips that might make your old one more comfortable.

For a mattress that's a little saggy, a bedboard placed between the mattress and the springs will provide support and firmness. A bedboard can be wood or pressed cardboard. You can buy cardboard ones in department stores or you can buy ½-inch (1-cm.) plywood cut to the right size at a lumberyard or building supply center. But if you have a couple of long shelf boards around that aren't being used, you can slip them under the mattress instead. You'll be amazed at how much difference this makes!

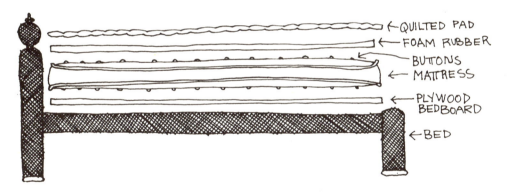

If you wake up feeling bruised all over from a lumpy mattress or from mattress buttons poking into you, a perfect solution is a pad of foam rubber. One-inch-thick (2- or 2½-cm.) foam rubber pads, cut to bed size, are available at most discount centers as well as some department stores. Even if the pad is for a bigger bed than you have, you can easily cut it to the right size with scissors. Put the foam rubber pad directly on top of the mattress and put the quilted cotton mattress pad on top of the foam. This makes it easy to change the bed, leaving the foam pad in place. These pads are not very expensive and you'll feel as if you have a whole new bed.

Even if there's nothing wrong with your mattress, you may be tired of the head and foot boards of your bed. You might be able to paint them but it could be more fun to give your room a whole new look. Put your bed on the floor! You can, of course, put just the mattress on the floor, but it will probably be more comfortable to put both the box spring and mattress on the floor together. Since you won't be able to vacuum under your bed anymore, be sure your floor is clean first. Then get an old contour sheet for the box spring. Put it on upside down so the sheet part is on the floor to protect the box spring from dirt. This also provides a neat cover for the side edges of the box spring.

Hide an Extra Bed!

You'll probably want an extra bed for overnight guests and you may even have an extra old mattress around the house but don't know where to put it in your room. One easy solution is to slide it under your own bed and then just slide it out when you need it. If you've put your bed on the floor, just make it another layer thicker by putting the extra mattress in the middle or on top. You can keep an old contour sheet or mattress cover on it all the time and that will make it easier to slide out when you need it.

If you can put your floor bed in a corner, you can turn the whole thing into a super study area. Instead of a bedspread, use a big, cheerful blanket or quilt or a colorful lightweight rug. You could even buy some of that fluffy, washable bathroom carpeting and cut it so it covers your bed. Then gather up a ton of comfy pillows (make your own, see page 88) and you have a cozy corner for yourself and your friends to study in or listen to records.

USING UNFINISHED FURNITURE
If you don't find what you want in used furniture, look at new unfinished furniture. It is very sturdy and usually made out of pine. There are bookcases, chests of drawers, desks, beds, cabinets, tables, chairs, in many different sizes. Unfinished furniture is not as inexpensive as it used to be, but it is still a lot cheaper than buying new finished furniture. Finishing it yourself can be fun. Besides paint and contact paper, you can use wood stains or varnish on unfinished furniture.

Wood stains look warm and attractive and are very easy to do. Just dip a wadded-up old rag into the stain and wipe it on the wood until it's the right color. Use plastic or rubber gloves, newspapers, and the same precautions as you do with paint, as stain is very hard to take out. And go lightly at first; you can always make it a little darker, but it really can't be lightened. Varnish is like clear, shiny paint and you can brush or spray it on over the plain raw wood or over dry stained wood to give the surface of your furniture a shiny protective finish.

MAKING YOUR OWN FURNITURE
Unless you are quite skilled at carpentry and have access to a variety of fancy tools, it's pretty hard to construct furniture out of plain wood. But there are a lot of things you can build easily by combining prefabricated units or things like cinder blocks and a few boards. None of these projects requires a saw; the

most you will need is a hammer and some nails or tacks and a tape measure.

Plywood and pressed wood can be bought at lumberyards or building supply stores. You may find it precut to the size you need, or you can have it cut to the exact size you want. Sometimes you can even find the wood you need in the scrap pile at the lumberyard; then it won't cost you anything.

Cardboard and fiberboard chests and file cabinets are available in five-and-ten-cent stores and many discount stores. This furniture is sturdier than you might think, and much cheaper than wood furniture.

Cardboard furniture can be painted or covered with contact paper in the same way as wood furniture or pieces of plywood. So when you've assembled your new pieces, you can decorate them however you want to match the rest of your room.

Here are some possibilities for combining these units to make your own furniture.

Board and Cinder-block Bookcase

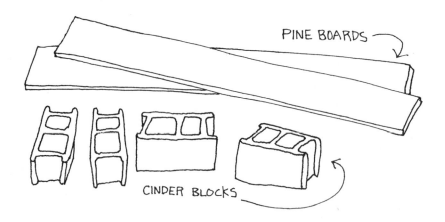

What You'll Need:
pine boards
cinder blocks
optional: spray paint, wood stain

It's really easy to build a bookcase out of boards and cinder blocks. And because it is open at both sides, you can stick it out into the room as a divider if you want.

Use foot-wide (30-cm.) pine boards and ask the lumberyard salesperson to cut them into the lengths you want. Cinder blocks are about 1 foot (30 cm.) long, and they come in a variety of designs. Look for them in a lumberyard or building supply store. You might want to stain the shelves and either leave the blocks natural or spray-paint them.

Make your bookcase as high as you like. You will need enough blocks for both ends of the bookcase, and if your boards are much more than 5 feet (1½ meters) long you should use supporting blocks in the middle too.

When building your bookcase, put pieces of cardboard under the bottom blocks so they won't scratch the floor. Also, if your floor slants a little you will need to put a couple of thicknesses of cardboard under the front of the bottom blocks to keep the bookcase leaning back firmly against the wall.

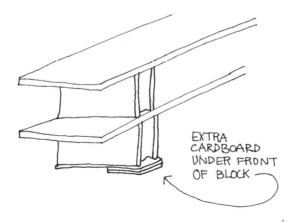
EXTRA CARDBOARD UNDER FRONT OF BLOCK

☆slapdash tip
Step Right Up!

Why not make a stepped bookcase? Just use shorter boards for the top one or two shelves. Then you can put the low end next to your bed for a combination night table and bookcase. Or you could make it an entertainment center, with records on the bottom shelf and your radio or record player on the low open end. For a bookcase with more than one step, you could put an aquarium at eye level and a tall potted plant on the lower end. The possibilities are endless!

Desk

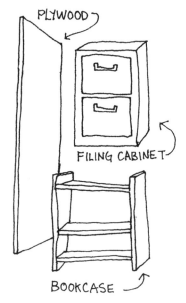

What You'll Need:
plywood rectangle
2 supports of the same height
contact paper, paint, or other decorative material

For a useful and good-looking desk, use a piece of ½-inch or ¾-inch (1-cm.) plywood supported at both ends by cardboard or wooden chests of drawers or file drawers. You could use one of each, or use a bookcase at one end instead of drawers; just make sure the two supports are the same height. In fact, you can use just about anything that's fairly sturdy for the desk supports. Wooden crates would make good storage places for books and records and so would low kitchen cabinets. You could even rest the desk top on two cinder-block and board bookshelves (see page 32).

The desk top can be about 4 to 5 feet long (1¼ to 1½ meters), depending on your space; if it's much longer it may sag in the middle! And its width should be the same as the depth of your supports or it will be unsteady and may tilt when you lean on it.

Contact paper makes a great washable surface for a desk. You may want to paint the supports, or even paint the whole desk in one or two colors. You could use contrasting paint or tape to label each drawer. Or what about covering the desk surface with a collage of sports photos from magazines or newspapers? Just glue them on with white glue and then cover with clear varnish, liquid polyurethane, spray plastic, or transparent contact paper. Then you could make a wine-bottle desk lamp (see page 106) and cover it with the same kind of pictures.

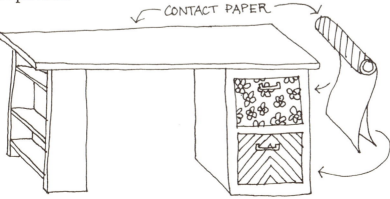

Vanity Dresser

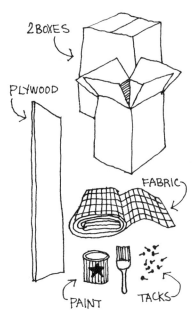

What You'll Need:
board or plywood rectangle
2 supports of the same height
paint or other decorative material
fabric
thumbtacks or upholstery tacks
optional: white glue, glass rectangle

You can make a glamorous vanity the same way you make a desk. Of course a vanity doesn't need to be as large as a desk. And you can use wooden or cardboard storage boxes (see page 47) as supports and then make a skirt to cover the front and sides.

If you plan to paint the vanity top and supports, do this first. For a skirt, choose material that goes with your décor, perhaps fabric you have used elsewhere in your room. Flowered or gingham-checked sheets would be perfect. Or you might even find an old pair of ruffled curtains packed away; if no one wants them, they will make a terrific vanity-table skirt. Just be sure to cut them so the ruffle will hang at the bottom of the skirt.

The skirt needs slit openings in front of the storage boxes or drawers so you can get at your things, and another in the middle for your legs. Make the skirt quite full so the slits will overlap and not show. You'll need fabric 1½ times as long as the measurement around the vanity where the skirt will hang. The top of your vanity will probably be around 28 to 32 inches (70–85 cm.) from the floor, so 36-inch-wide material (90-cm.) will work fine. Fold under the edge at the top so the bottom edge just clears the floor. Using thumbtacks or fancy upholstery tacks, tack the ends of the fabric to the back corners of the

SLIT FOR KNEES
SLITS FOR ACCESS TO STORAGE BOXES

vanity top edge. Then find the middle of the fabric and tack that to the middle of the front edge of the vanity. Now tack the rest of the fabric to the vanity, making small pleats to use up the excess material. Make the same number of pleats on each side. Then slit the fabric up from the floor almost to the top in front of the storage supports and in the middle where you'll sit.

To cover the vanity top, you can spread a thin layer of white glue all over it and then smooth down a piece of the same fabric you used for the skirt. Then, if you like, add a piece of glass cut by a glazier to exactly the same size as the vanity top. A glass top is both elegant and practical since it's easy to clean. And how about making your vanity top into a giant scrapbook by putting your favorite photos and mementos under the glass!

☆ slapdash tip
Mirror, Mirror on the Wall

Every vanity needs a mirror, of course! Yours could be an old one from the basement or a secondhand store, or you might find an inexpensive new one at the dime store. To complete your vanity set, cut strips of the skirt fabric to cover the frame and glue them on with white glue; make the strips wide enough to go around the frame and glue the edges down at the back.

If you want to be really fancy, make a ruffle around the frame (see page 80). Then hang the mirror over the vanity—be sure to sit down to find the right height for it. Hanging instructions are on page 100.

Vanity Stool

UNFINISHED WOODEN STOOL

What You'll Need:
unfinished wooden stool
fabric
thumbtacks or upholstery tacks

What about making a stool to match your new vanity? It's really simple. Buy an unfinished stool about 18 inches (45 cm.) high at a building supply center or unfinished furniture store. They are quite sturdy and are not expensive.

Cut a circle of fabric 45 inches (112 cm.) in diameter; use pinking shears if you have them so the cut edge won't ravel. (An easy way to make a circle is to cut your fabric in a square 45 inches (112 cm.) on each side. Then fold this square once in each direction to make a small square four layers thick. On the two sides that are not folded, cut an arc across from one corner to the corner diagonally opposite. Then open up the circle.)

Place the center of the fabric circle on the center of the stool seat. Drape the fabric evenly over all sides and pull it smooth across the seat. Hold it in place with tacks around the edge of the seat.

Of course you can decorate the vanity stool cover and the vanity skirt any way you like if the fabric doesn't look exciting enough by itself. Use rickrack, fringe, bobbles, or any other trim from the notions counter along the edges, or tack fluttery pieces of fancy ribbon to the top edge and let them hang down at different lengths. For a really gorgeous effect, tie a wide satin ribbon around the edge of the seat in a fancy bow; be sure to tack the ribbon in a few places so it won't be dislodged.

☆ slapdash tip
Comfort Counts!

If you spend a lot of time looking in the mirror, you may want to make your vanity stool more comfortable! You can make a separate cushion to fit the seat; cover it with the skirt fabric (see p. 90). But a much easier method is to cut a circle to fit the seat from a foam rubber pad or an old mattress pad. Then drape and tack the skirt fabric right over it (be sure to cut the skirt fabric a little longer if the pad is thick).

Night Table

What You'll Need:
unfinished wooden stool
circle of pressed wood
fabric
hammer and nails

It's convenient to have a table beside your bed for your lamp and book and a clock. You can easily make a terrific round table from a precut circle of pressed wood and a stool. This table will also come in very handy as a game table or for snacks with your friends, as it is fairly sturdy and can be moved easily. Look for the pressed wood circle at a lumberyard or discount building supply store. They are already cut in different sizes so you can get whatever size you think will go well in your room. Don't get an expensive wood circle as it will be covered anyway; a cheap pressed wood one is fine. You'll probably be able to buy the wooden stool at the same place. Unfinished four-legged stools come in different heights, so choose one that will be easy to reach from your bed.

You will also need 3 or 4 heavy 2½-inch (6-cm.) nails and a hammer. Center the pressed wood circle on the top of the stool and nail it down in several places.

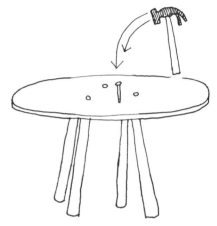

You don't have to bother painting this table because you will cover it with a circular cloth. Choose a washable, permanent-press fabric—sheet fabric is ideal. You could use the same fabric you've used elsewhere, or you might want to use a contrasting color or design. For example, a scenic print might look great. To make the cloth, measure from the center of your new table top across the edge and down to the floor. You need a square of material twice this distance on all four sides. Then fold and cut the fabric in a circle the same way you did for the vanity stool (see page 39). If you like you can sew fringe or a ruffle to the top or bottom edge of the cloth. Just make sure it's washable so the whole cloth can be thrown in the washing machine now and then.

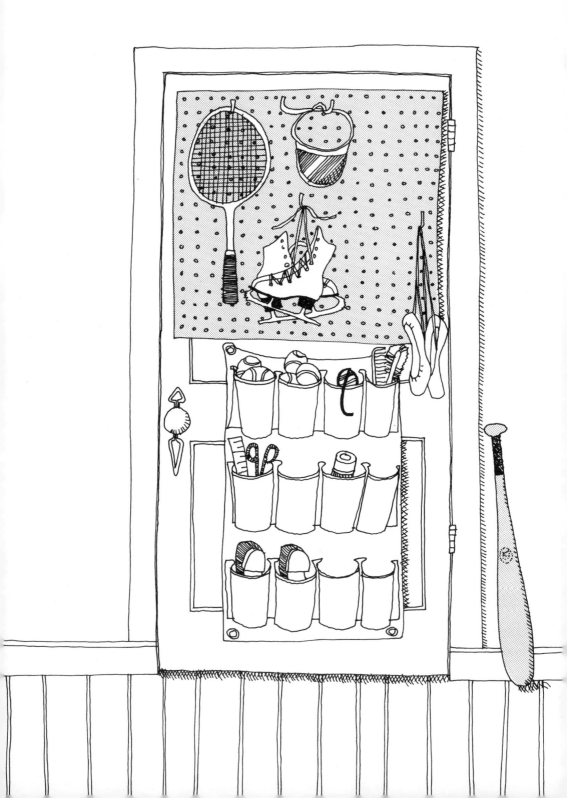

Closets and Storage Space

ORGANIZING YOUR CLOSET

Storage space is often a problem and many closets are not designed well enough to hold all they should. But you can probably get a lot more of your gear into your closet with a bit of planning. Here are a few ideas to help you get started.

If your closet rod is quite high, there's probably a lot of empty and unusable space below your hanging clothes. Try adding a lower rod across your closet. A tension rod (the kind with a spring built in so it doesn't need brackets to hold it up) can be found in most hardware or building supply stores. If you can't find one you can use a regular rod and brackets, but it will be harder to move it up or down if you change your mind.

Depending on the shape of your closet, you could put your new rod directly under the old one for two layers of hanging clothes. Or you could add one or two rods across the ends of your closet at right angles to the old rod. And see if you can work out a design using storage cubes (see page 47) on the closet floor. Even two or three cubes will hold a lot of heavy things (like ice skates) and will help you to organize your space.

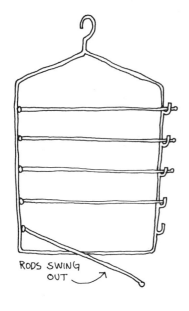

RODS SWING OUT

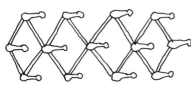

Of course, hooks, hanging shoe bags, plastic sweater boxes, and other closet accessories can do a lot to help organize your storage area. A multiple pants hanger with swinging rods need not be used for pants. It can hold a lot of purses or neckties or winter scarves. Browse through the dime store for other convenient organizers; a kitchen utensil rack or a row of cup hooks might be perfect for the inside of your closet door. Another inexpensive "hang up" is a wooden mug rack or hat rack. Hanging on the *outside* of your closet door or on the wall, it's both useful and decorative when you drape it with costume jewelry, hair ribbons, and colorful sashes.

☆ slapdash tip

A Loopy Idea

To hold all your belts or necklaces, make a giant "key ring" loop from a wire clothes hanger. Use a pliers to untwist the ends and to straighten the whole hanger, including the hook. (If you want a smaller loop, bend the wire back and forth with the pliers at the point where you want to break it until it falls off.) Now bend the wire into a big circle; with the pliers, bend back a little of the wire at the ends so you can hook them together.

String on all your loose belts and dangly

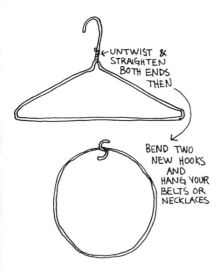

UNTWIST & STRAIGHTEN BOTH ENDS THEN

BEND TWO NEW HOOKS AND HANG YOUR BELTS OR NECKLACES

items and loop the whole ring over the closet rod or a wall hook. Now you can easily get at whichever belt you need without searching behind all the stuff on the floor!

A good way to keep lightweight but bulky items together is a drawstring bag. If you don't have one, you can make one the size you need out of any cheerful fabric that is washable and fairly sturdy. Just cut out two rectangles the same size and turn under an inch or so (2½ cm.) at one short end of each piece for a casing. Sew these casings by machine or with firm hand stitching. Then, with right sides together, stitch the other three edges together, stopping the stitching where the casing begins on each side. Thread a piece of old clothesline or other rope through the casings. Make the drawstring long enough so you can open the bag to get your stuff in and out.

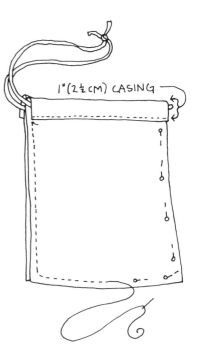

Handy Hang Ups

Is your closet so messy that it needs emergency assistance? A really simple system for storing bulky lightweight items is a collection of fancy paper shopping bags. Label them in big letters with paint or colored tape. Then you can find what you need at a glance—leotards, camping clothes, winter socks, craft materials, fabric for sewing projects, and even outgrown clothes for the rummage sale!

To hang up these bags as well as lots of other goodies, cup hooks or other hooks will work fine. But it's more fun to attach a pegboard to your closet door. And with pegboard you can move things around any time.

You can buy pegboard at most discount building supply stores or lumberyards. Have it cut to the size you need and tell the salesperson what kind of door you are hanging it on. Pegboard is usually attached with nails, molly bolts, or mirror clips. The person who sells you the pegboard will be able to help you choose the best way to put it on your closet door.

Why not paint your pegboard—you could make stripes or wild patterns on it to brighten up your closet. Be sure to let the paint dry completely before attaching the board to your closet door.

Then get a package of assorted hooks so you'll have just what you need for your "hang ups." You might even want to hang a small shoe bag (the kind with rows of pockets) from the bottom of your pegboard. Fill the pockets with all those small items (like your shoe brush, spot remover, tennis balls, etc.) that always seem to be lost. You'll know now just where to find them.

Building a Storage Unit

What You'll Need:
corrugated cardboard cartons (all the same size)
masking tape
paint or other decorative material
optional: small pieces of thin cardboard and fabric for lining

No one ever seems to have enough storage space, and often the space you have is the wrong shape or size. But you can make an easy and inexpensive set of stacking cubes that's designed for your own storage needs. Best of all, you can be as wildly creative as you want when you decorate it.

You will need corrugated cardboard cartons all of the same size. The best source for clean and sturdy cartons is a place that sells wine or liquor. These stores always have empty case cartons and they are usually happy to get rid of them. Find out what day the store gets its deliveries so you can get a number of clean boxes of the same brand. They will probably all be the same size. The number of boxes you need depends on how big a storage unit you want. And don't throw out those nifty divider panels until after you get home, because you may want to use them.

When you have the boxes in your room you can start stacking and arranging them. Some may still have their covers cut only on three sides. Don't cut these off yet—you may want to use them for covered storage space. If you decide to put your storage unit against a wall, you will want to put all the boxes on their sides with the open ends facing out. But if you need a room divider, make one with your storage unit. Just stack the boxes so that some open onto one side of the room and some onto the other. This is especially good for two people who share a room—you both get storage space in the room divider.

When your storage unit is stacked up, use masking tape to tape the boxes together where they meet. Use two or three pieces of masking tape across the edges that meet. You can then put a wide strip of masking tape over the open "seams" so that you will have flat sides and top when you paint.

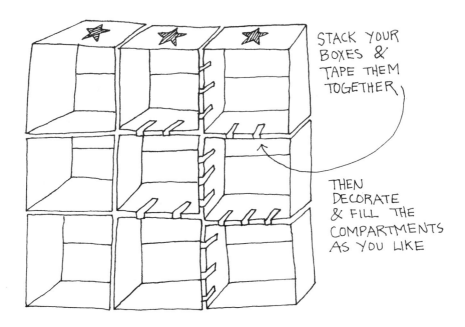

Before you paint or decorate the whole unit, decide where you want to use the cardboard dividers that came in the boxes. If you knit or crochet, these dividers make a perfect place to keep your yarns. Small pieces of other hobby equipment, such as models, can be organized and kept safe in these dividers.

If you are using dividers in some of the storage cubes, you'll have to decide on your color scheme before you tape them inside the boxes. When you've decided on colors, paint the insides of the boxes and the dividers you're using in them. Secure the dividers to the insides of the boxes when all the paint is dry.

Now you're ready to decorate the insides of the rest of the boxes and the outside of the unit. Let your imagination run wild. Combine paint, contact paper, felt, decals, and colored tape to try any look you think you'll like. The worst that can happen is that you'll want to do it over or start with new boxes, and the best will be a creative design that's uniquely yours. If you're sports-car minded, your whole unit could look like a speedy car with racing stripes! Or maybe you'll end up with a graphic of blue skies and restful clouds.

Those flap lids can be left on some of the boxes to keep your collection safe from dust and prying eyes. Maybe you'll want to paint labels, directions, or invitations on the flaps that cover your treasures.

☆slapdash tip

Show Off Something Special! Wouldn't you love to have an elegant fabric-lined cubbyhole to display your most prized possessions? It's very easy to make one. Cut pieces of cardboard (sides of other boxes will be fine) that exactly fit all of the inner walls of the cubbyhole. Then cut pieces of fabric a little larger than the cardboard pieces. Stretch the fabric across one side of each cardboard piece and tape the fabric edges to the other side. Then carefully slide the pieces inside the box for a neatly lined storage area.

When you are deciding what to put in your storage cubes, keep in mind that putting heavy things in the bottom sections will give the unit more stability. Very heavy things should go only on the very bottom so the boxes won't cave in.

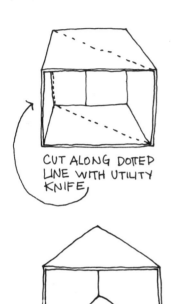

CUT ALONG DOTTED LINE WITH UTILITY KNIFE

STACK A NUMBER OF THESE "CORNER CUBES" FOR A NEAT DISPLAY AREA

☆slapdash tip

Create a Corner Cupboard!
Maybe you've been wondering what to do with that unused corner of your room where nothing seems to fit. A corner storage hutch may be the perfect answer. Just cut the corrugated cardboard cubes in half diagonally with a utility knife; then stack and decorate them as on page 47. This hutch makes a super display case for a collection and it will brighten up that dreary corner of your room.

Making a Storage Chest/Window Seat

What You'll Need:
foot locker or trunk-type chest
paint or other decorative material
optional: pillows for top; fabric and upholstery tacks or Velcro for skirt

Many homes have old and ugly storage chests and foot lockers stashed away in the basement or attic. Rescue one of these forlorn items and turn it into a terrific bench or window seat. The extra storage space for your room is a bonus!

Clean the chest thoroughly inside and out. If it has mildew, remove this with some chlorine laundry bleach in water and then put the chest out in the sun or in a well-ventilated area to dry completely.

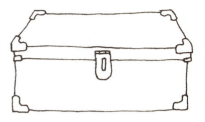

You can paint your chest and then make cushions to fit the top (see page 88). Or you can just paint the lid and make a skirt to cover the sides and front of the chest the same way you made the vanity skirt (see page 36). Try using paint to match your desk or dresser and fabric to match your curtains.

For a wooden chest, attach the skirt to the sides and front with a line of fancy upholstery tacks just under the lid. For a metal chest, run a line of stitching across the top of the skirt to hold the pleats. Then glue Velcro strips or dots to the chest and sew corresponding Velcro to the inside of the skirt.

Your chest might look great at the foot of your bed; a low one is probably the perfect height for a bed that's on the floor. You could also put it under the window with a group of plants or stuffed animals on top. Or forget the cushions for the lid and use the chest as a nightstand.

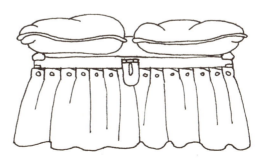

Windows

The first thing to figure out is how you want to cover your window. You might want the simplicity and clean design of a shade. Or you might decide on the softer and more elaborate look of curtains or drapes. Perhaps your window doesn't really need any cover, and what you really want is something to make it look attractive and less stark. Why not try hanging plants at different heights in front of the window and adding one or two on the windowsill?

Make a Window Display!

You can turn your whole window into a super setting for your choicest odds and ends. Buy bracket strips—the metal kind that have a vertical row of little holes to put the brackets in that hold the shelves. Attach these strips to both sides of your window, making sure the holes for the brackets are lined up evenly so the shelves will be level. Light boards or glass are fine for shelves; be sure they are the right width for the brackets you choose, and are long enough to reach across the whole window. Then set up your display. A collection of models and sports trophies or a potpourri of pretty bottles, glass figures, and small plants will look sensational with the light shining through them.

Think about the amount of light that comes through your windows and also about how drafty they are in winter. A window shade does a good job of keeping out light but not much for keeping out drafts. Heavy curtains or drapes will keep out both. Lightweight café curtains or shirred curtains would be a good choice for a room that doesn't get much light or draft. Another advantage of café curtains is that you can open the top ones to let in light and keep the bottom ones closed for privacy. Of course, you can combine a shade or blinds with any kind of curtain. Choose whatever fabric goes best with your décor. You could use the same fabric in several ways in your room, like for curtains and a comforter or a cloth cover for your night table. Or you could use one print for your curtains and a coordinated print or solid for other items in your room.

Mirror Magic

What can you possibly do with a dreary, unattractive window that doesn't even let in much light? Try some mirror magic! Glue strips of Mylar (mirror-surfaced plastic, available in plastic supply or wallpaper stores) around the inside of the window frame and along the sill; you'll be amazed at how much more light and excitement will bounce into your room!

Another trick is to glue adhesive-backed mirror squares (available in building supply stores) to the wall all around the window—this makes a reflecting frame.

A less expensive way to make that dull

window an interesting focal point for your room is to paint a frame (about 4 inches or 10 cm. wide) on the wall around it (be sure to ask first if this will be okay). Frame the window in a color that echoes one you've used elsewhere, perhaps in your rug or bedspread.

DECORATING READY-MADE SHADES

Plain white roll-up shades are inexpensive (get them at a discount store) and very easy to install (just follow the directions). You can decorate them as much or as little as you like. Fringe or bobbles can be bought in strips at any notions counter and glued or stapled along the bottom edge. And, of course, you can make a fancy pull with ribbon or embroidered tape or braided yarn.

The shade itself can be decorated with paint, felt-tip pens, decals, or collages of cut-out pictures. Just be sure that anything you glue to the shade is completely flat and not lumpy; it must be securely glued all over and especially around the edges or it will get crumpled when you roll up the shade. Any design that goes with your room is fine; you could try painting stripes or an interesting over-all pattern.

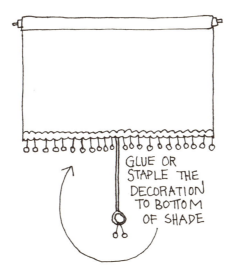
GLUE OR STAPLE THE DECORATION TO BOTTOM OF SHADE

OR PAINT A NICE SCENE

☆ slapdash tip

Choose Your Own View!

How about painting your window shade with the scene you'd like to see out your window—a field of flowers, a cow, a football field? Or you could use masking tape to make stencils. Just put the tape in place, paint over the whole thing (outdoors or on lots of newspaper), and then lift off the tape for the design. And don't forget the neighbors—why not put a smiling face or a moon or a sleeping figure on the outside of the shade!

Making Your Own Shades

What You'll Need:
shade roller and slat
brackets (if necessary)
fabric
thumbtacks
needle and thread
shade pull

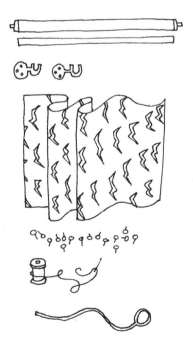

It's quite simple and inexpensive to make your own fabric window shades. You just need to be cautious about the fabric you choose. Tightly woven, fairly heavy cottons will keep out light and won't ravel. Cotton duck (the striped kind that some outdoor sling chairs are made

56

of) or lightweight canvas works very well. You can buy window shade rollers at most large hardware or building supply stores and, of course, at a shade and window blind shop. Be sure to get brackets at the same time if you need them, and get a slat for the bottom edge of the shade.

Cut out a rectangle of fabric *exactly* as wide as the wood part of the roller and about 18 inches (45 cm.) longer than your window. If the material is exactly the same width as the shade you plan to make, you are in luck—the selvage edges along the sides will keep the shade from raveling. You can't hem the side edges of window shades. If the fabric is too wide, cut *both* side edges to the width you need; you can't use one selvage edge and one cut edge or the shade will not roll up and down evenly. It's important that all four edges of fabric are cut straight.

Use thumbtacks to attach the top edge of the fabric securely straight across the wooden shade roller. Roll up the shade carefully so it is smooth and put it in the brackets. Pull it up and down a few times. You may find that the wrong side of fabric faces into your room or that the shade doesn't roll up evenly. If so, retack it at the top until it is right. Then just make a hem across the bottom edge of the shade big enough so you can slip the slat into it. Buy or make a pull and tack it through the shade fabric into the center of the slat.

Shirred Curtains

What You'll Need:
fabric
needle and thread
1 or 2 spring rods
optional: material for tiebacks, sewing machine

The easiest kind of curtains to make is shirred curtains. All you need to do is make a hem at the top edge of the fabric and push a rod through the hem; then slide the fabric along so its fullness is evenly distributed across the rod. Choose a lightweight fabric. For each window you need a piece of fabric about 6 inches (15 cm.) longer than the window (to allow for hems) and 1½ to 2 times as wide as the window (for fullness). If you just want to cover the window but are not really concerned about keeping light or drafts out, you can use lightweight fabrics like voile or Indian gauze. Sheet fabric will also work well.

Buy a rod that is the width of your window. The easiest kind to install, as well as the least expensive, is a spring-type rod that has little rubber caps at each end. The spring inside the rod holds it against the sides of the window frame. If you'd rather have your curtains shirred at both top and bottom, buy two rods for each window.

Cut your curtain fabric in half lengthwise (so the curtain

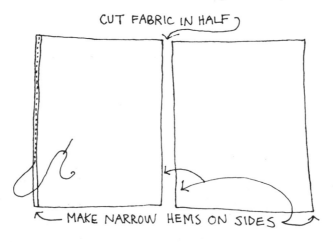

will open at the center) and make narrow hems along all the raw side edges. Now turn under about 1½ inches (4 cm.) at the top and make a line of firm hand or machine stitching for a casing. Slide the rod through the casings of both pieces, bunching up the fabric to make it fit. Put the rod in place and then pin up as much of the curtain as is necessary for the bottom hem or casing. (If you are using a rod at the bottom, make the casing so the fabric will be pulled fairly taut when the rods are installed.)

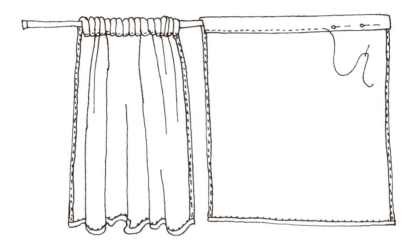

For top-shirred curtains you may want to make tiebacks. These are strips of fabric that go around the curtain and attach to the wall or edge of the window frame to pull the curtains back (see page 66). Make the tiebacks out of the same or a contrasting fabric, wide ribbon, embroidered tape, fancy cord, or whatever else will look good in your room. If you use ribbon or tape, you could add a band of the same ribbon to decorate the bottom edge of your curtains.

☆ slapdash tip

Preserve Your Privacy!

If you have an open closet or a wardrobe with no door, cover it with a shirred curtain. Or use one to make a closet out of an alcove in your room. Get a spring rod the right size and hang the curtains from the top of the doorway to the floor. You can even use a piece of string or cord instead of a rod and then just tack the ends to the inside of the doorway after you've put it through the casing of the curtains.

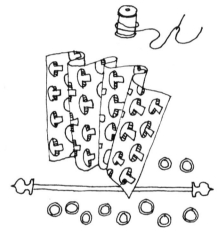

Café Curtains

What You'll Need:
fabric
spring or café curtain rods
café curtain rings
needle and thread
optional: rickrack or other decorative trim, sewing machine

Café curtains hang from the center rather than the top of the window. The top edge is usually gathered into pleats. A ring is attached to each pleat and the rings slide along the curtain rod. You can also make another set of café curtains for the top half of the windows. Or you can use a shirred valance at the top of the window if you prefer.

You can use either spring rods or café curtain rods that hang out from the wall on brackets. Buy them at any hardware or department store. You'll probably see quite a selection to choose from; café rods may be made of gold-colored metal or plain or painted wood. They come in various thicknesses, and have different kinds of fancy ends. Get a kind that will go well with the rest of your room. Also buy a package of rings for each curtain. You can get rings that clip onto the fabric pleats or the kind that must be sewn on—the clip-on kind is, of course, faster to use. Be sure the rings are large enough to slide on the rods.

Café curtains can be made out of either light or moderately heavy fabric. You might be able to use a border print fabric if the material is wide enough for the length of the curtain. Of course, you can trim your curtains with a band of decorative tape, rickrack, or ribbon sewn near the bottom.

You need a rectangle of fabric about 6 inches (15 cm.) longer and twice as wide as the section of window you are going to cover. Cut the fabric in half so your curtains will open in the middle. Then make narrow hems on any side edges that are not selvage edges. Make a 4-inch (10-cm.) hem along the top edges of the curtains. Use a straight line of machine or hand stitching. Now you are ready to make your pleats. Starting 2 inches (5 cm.) in from one side, make a pencil or chalk mark every 4 inches (10 cm.) along the top hem on the right side of the

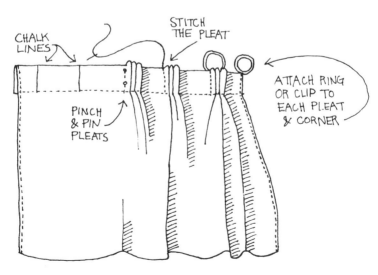

curtains. Use a ruler to make lines straight down from the top of the curtain to the edge of the hem at each mark you've made. Starting at the first pencil line, pinch the fabric up in three even pinches that end at the second pencil mark. Pin through these pleats along the pencil lines. Move along to the next two pencil marks (leaving a flat space) and do the same thing. Do this all the way across. You will have about a 4-inch (10-cm.) space between each set of pleats. Now, using a machine or very firm hand stitching, sew through all the layers of fabric in each pleat. Make your line of stitching straight down from the top of the curtain to the end of the top hem. Clip or sew a ring to the top of each set of pleats and to each end corner. Then string your curtains on the rod. After the rod is in place, pin up the lower edge of the curtain so it hangs evenly where you want it to end. Hem and press. Add whatever decorations you want now.

Make an upper set of café curtains the same way. Or, if you don't need real curtains to cover the top of the window, make a valance by shirring a 4 to 6 inch (10–15 cm.) strip of fabric (see page 59).

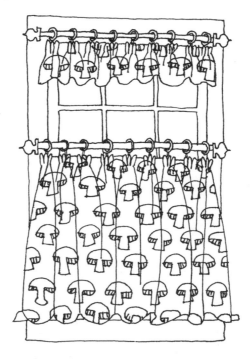

Full-length Curtains or Drapes

What You'll Need:
fabric
regular curtain rod and curtain rings *or* traverse rod, pleater tape and hooks
needle and thread
optional: sewing machine

If you don't have traverse rods (the kind that open and close your drapes when you pull a cord at the side), you can make drapes or full-length curtains the same way you did café curtains. Use a regular curtain rod mounted on brackets. A spring rod won't hold full-length curtains unless they are very lightweight.

An even simpler way to make full-length curtains is to get material that is only a little wider than your windows. Then cut the material in half lengthwise and hem the top and sides of each piece, if necessary. Attach rings to the top every 4 inches (10 cm.) or so. Slide the rings over a spring rod or regular curtain rod and hem the bottom of the curtains to the right length. When these curtains are closed they don't have the full drapy effect of pleated curtains and the top will hang down in shallow dips between the rings. But this effect can look quite nice with plain but textured fabric like burlap. And when these curtains are open they hang a lot like pleated ones.

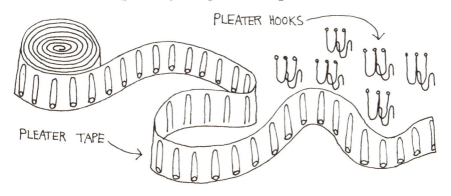

Making drapes to hang on traverse rods is also quite easy. But you need to buy "pleater tape." This is sold in the drapery section of fabric or department stores. The salesperson can help you decide how much tape and how many hooks as well as how much fabric you need if you take your window and rod measurements with you. To sew on the pleater tape and stick in the hooks, just follow the directions.

"Fake" Curtains or Drapes

What You'll Need:
fabric
regular curtain rods, spring rods, or cup hooks
needle and thread
optional: curtain rings, sewing machine

FAKE CURTAINS HUNG WITH CUPHOOKS

Fake drapes are strips of fabric that hang just inside the edges of the window frame. They can't open or close. But these fake drapes can add a terrific accent to your room, and they cost much less because they don't need as much material as real drapes.

You may have found some super bold print or textured fabric that's too expensive for regular drapes. A remnant of this material might be enough for fake drapes or a valance. This is also a good way to use quilted or other very heavy fabric that would be too bulky for regular drapes. Or you might have some fabric left over from making a floor pillow or comforter that would look great at your window too.

Each fake drape should be about 1½ to 2 feet wide (45–60 cm.), although for a small window they can be narrower. Hem the drapes at the top. Then slide them over a rod or attach rings to them. You could even hang them with rings from two or three cup hooks screwed into the top of the window frame at each side; put the hooks close together so the fabric will hang well. Hang the drapes and pin up the bottoms to the right length, then hem. When the drapes are bunched up at the top, they will hang in loose draped folds.

These drapes look great over a window shade or shirred curtains. Tiebacks and valances give an even more finished look.

Make Your Window More Important!
Extend the size of your window with side panels and a decorative rod! Buy a fancy rod, or one with fancy fittings on the ends, that complements the look of your room.

But be sure the rod is a couple of feet or so (⅔ meter) longer than the window is wide. Then mount the rod (the hardware comes with it) so that it extends beyond the window frame an equal distance on both sides. Attach the fake drapes to several big rings and hang them from the rod at each side of the window.

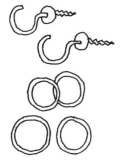

Tiebacks

What You'll Need:
fabric strips
cup hooks
4 small metal or plastic rings
needle and thread

ATTACH RING TO ONE END, TEST THE LENGTH, THEN ATTACH OTHER RING

Ribbon or fancy tape or cord can, of course, be used as tiebacks for curtains. But you may want to make tiebacks out of your curtain fabric. They should be about 3 to 4 inches wide (7½–10 cm.). Start out with a strip about 1½ feet long (45 cm.). Use pinking shears along the raw edges or make narrow hems. Screw a cup hook into the edge of the window frame on each side of the window at the height you want your tiebacks. You need 4 small metal or plastic rings for each pair of tiebacks; buy them at a hardware or dime store or in the drapery department of a fabric store. Sew a ring to one end of each tieback and then hook the ring to the cup hook. Gather the curtain in your hands and put the tieback around it. When you have decided how tight you want your tiebacks, cut off any excess material from the end of the tieback and sew a ring to this end too.

Of course, rope, ribbon, or embroidered tape tiebacks can just be tied in a knot and looped over the cup hook.

Valances

What You'll Need:
fabric
spring rod or thumbtacks or pushpins
needle and thread

Valances are decorative pieces of fabric across the tops of windows. They can give a dramatic look to windows or make one window a more important focal point for the room. You can make a valance plain or fancy; you could add fringe, scallop the top or bottom edge, make a shirred valance for a ruffled effect, or anything else that appeals to you. Or how about making a valance and tiebacks out of a fabric that contrasts with your curtains?

If you have a valance board at the top of your window, tack your valance material to it. Otherwise, hang a valance either on the outside upper edge of the window frame, using thumbtacks or pushpins, or

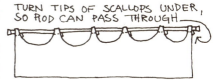

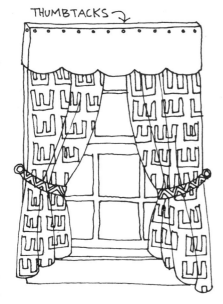

from a spring rod at the upper inner edge of the window frame. If you use a spring rod, make a casing by hemming the top edge of the valance so the rod can slide through. If you scalloped the top edge, turn the tips of the scallops under so the rod can go through them. To hang a valance with tacks on the outside of the window frame, just make sure the valance is wide enough to go all the way around the frame to meet the wall—this will give a more finished, boxlike look. This kind of valance will hang over the top of your regular or fake curtains.

Cut your valances neatly and don't bother to hem them at the bottom or sides; they won't ravel because you never pull or move them once they're up.

Decorative Shower Curtain

What You'll Need:
fabric
stapler
needle and thread

You can even carry your decorating scheme into the bathroom. Besides shirred curtains at the window (see page 58) and an interesting-looking wastebasket (see page 108), you can easily make a decorative outer shower curtain. An outer shower curtain is just fabric that hangs outside the tub in front of the waterproof shower curtain hanging inside the tub. Cut the fabric the same size as the regular shower curtain. Hem the side and bottom edges if necessary. Then cut scallops along the top edge so that the points of the scallops come up between the holes for hooks in the regular shower curtain. Staple these points to the top edge of the regular shower curtain so the scallops fall beneath the hooks, and you'll suddenly have a new and exciting-looking bathroom.

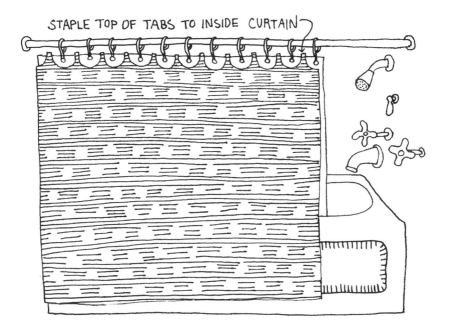

Bed Coverings

Because your bed is probably the largest thing in your room, whatever you cover it with will be a very important element of your decorating scheme. So think about the effect you'd like—sporty, elegant, or wildly dramatic. Also consider how you use your room; if you always have a gang of friends flopping on the bed and everywhere else, you'll need something that can take a lot of wear and tear. And if you like to read or study on your bed, munching popcorn or potato chips, make sure to choose something washable!

Remember that you're going to see a lot of whatever fabric you use to cover your bed. Choose something that goes well with the other things you want in the room, like the curtains and the rug. It doesn't have to match or be the same fabric or even the same design. You're aiming for a really terrific over-all look. But keep in mind that some prints or colors will look great covering a large area like a bed, and others probably won't. If you have some fabric that you'd love to use but it's a little overwhelming for the whole bed, make a pillow or two out of it (see page 88). You could even cover your bed with a mountain of pillows of different patterns and colors.

TRANSFORMING AN OLD BEDSPREAD
Buying a new bedspread is an expensive undertaking, so if you have one that's in good shape, think about how you can jazz it up for a new look. If it's a plain color, the sky is the limit. You can use strips of trim around the edges, in stripes or windowpane patterns, or use it to write your name in block letters. A plain cotton spread can be painted with fabric paint, which you can find in a large paint or building supply store. Just be sure you plan your design in advance, because this paint is indelible. You could make a stenciled design by using masking

tape to block off the letters or patterns you don't want painted. Then spray on the paint (outdoors or with lots of newspaper all over) and peel off the masking tape when the paint is dry.

A print spread can be transformed by sewing on a large rectangular patch of plain color-coordinated fabric that just covers the top of the bed without hanging down the sides. (This is also a great solution if you've spilled hot chocolate in the middle of the spread!) Or use several different fabrics to make smaller patchwork-type squares or stripes. A flower print or something similar might look nice with the addition of ruffles or plain-colored ribbon along the edges. Even a collection of brightly colored pillows can change the whole look of your bed covering. You can recover pillows yourself quite easily (see page 88).

However, if what you really need is a whole new bedspread, read on!

Super Easy Bedspread

What You'll Need:
a fancy flat top sheet (same size as your bed)
a matching set of fancy pillowcases

A pretty and inexpensive way to cover your bed for summer is to use a fancy ruffled sheet and matching ruffled pillowcases. Buy a top sheet that is the right size for your bed. The trick is to put the ruffle, which is meant to go at the top of the bed, at the foot of your bed, almost touching the floor! When you lay the sheet on your bed this way, the other end will come just to the head of the mattress. Then the pillows in their matching pillowcases are plumped up against the head of the bed. It looks terrific, it's easy to wash, and when winter comes you can use it as a regular sheet. It's also light enough to leave on the bed all night. And, of course, it's easy to use another sheet of the same pattern to make curtains, a skirt for a vanity, or a cloth to cover your night table.

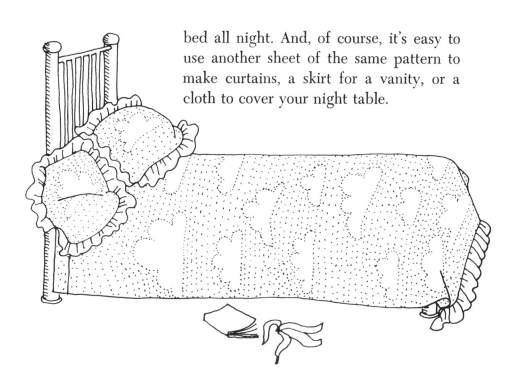

☆ slapdash tip

Spread Some Paint Around!

You can even design your own sheet-bedspread! Use a plain white or pastel sheet and plain pillowcases. Spray fabric paint over a masking-tape stencil on the sheet and pillowcases. (This paint, made especially for use on fabric, is available in paint or home building supply stores.) You might want to do your name in big block letters, or a picture, or a wild abstract design. Whatever you do, you will end up with a bedspread that is uniquely yours.

Making a Bedspread

What You'll Need:
3 pieces of fabric
needle and thread
optional: decorative trim

It's easy to make your own bedspread. And you can use almost any fabric you like. Of course, fabric that is sturdy and washable is best. Think about how corduroy, denim, or a bright heavy cotton would look in your room. What about patchwork or quilted fabric? Or you could even use fake fur! Since most fabric isn't wide enough to go all the way across your bed from the floor on one side to the floor on the other, you are going to use three strips of fabric. One strip will be as wide as the top of your bed and the other two will hang down from the side edges of your bed to the floor. You could even mix fabrics. Perhaps you'd like to use one for the top that is too expensive to use all over, and use another fabric that goes with it for the sides.

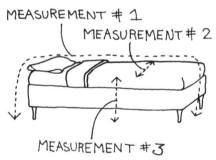

Measure from the floor at the foot of your bed up and over the bed all the way to the floor at the head of your bed. Then measure across your bed from one edge to the other, and add an inch or so (2½ cm.) to the width for seams. You will need one strip this size. Now measure from the edge of the bed down to the floor, and add 1 inch (2½ cm.) to this number. You need two more strips as long as the first strip and as wide as the measurement you just made.

Lay your fabric on your bed before you sew, to make sure it's right. Then just pin the side pieces to the top piece with right sides together. Be sure to use the selvage edges for the bottoms of the side pieces so you won't need to hem them. Use a machine or firm hand stitches to sew the three pieces together. Make narrow hems at the ends.

If you decide to add trim to your bedspread, you could use the same trim you've used elsewhere in your room. Sew a couple of bands of rickrack or tape around the edge near the bottom, or sew wide ribbon or tape across the middle to form the letters of your name.

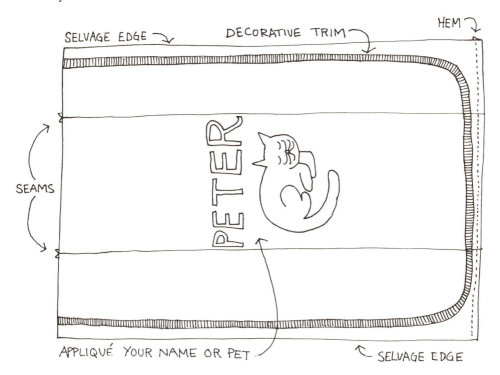

Comforter

What You'll Need:
1 flat sheet (your bed size)
1 or 2 packages of polyester quilt batting
sewing machine or needle and thread

Besides a super easy summer bedspread (page 72), sheets can make a great bed covering for winter. If you use matching sheets on the bed or as curtains, this will be an easy way to have a really coordinated look that costs much less than the ready-made components.

For a twin bed, one flat twin sheet will be plenty of fabric for a cozy comforter. Buy a sheet or two of polyester batting for the inside of your comforter. (One is enough; but you might want it fuller and fatter. If so, use two.) This batting is available at most large fabric stores. Make sure you get a sheet, not strips or shreds; the sheets come in standard sizes, usually 81" × 96".

Lay the batting flat on the floor. Fold the sheet in half with right sides out so the two shorter edges come together. Lay the folded sheet on the batting so two sides and a corner match up. Cut the batting to make a rectangle about 1 inch (2½ cm.) smaller each way than the folded sheet. (If you are using two sheets of batting, lay one on top of the other and cut them together.)

Open up the sheet and lay the cut batting on one half of it; the edges of the batting should be ½ inch (1 cm.) or so in from the edges of the sheet. If there's enough batting left over, you can cut it in large pieces and lay them on the first piece to make almost another whole layer. Now fold the other half of the

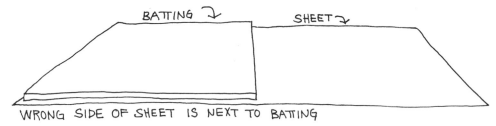
WRONG SIDE OF SHEET IS NEXT TO BATTING

sheet over the batting so the right sides of the sheet are facing out. Straighten it so it lies flat and pin all the layers together around all four edges. Put several pins in the middle part of the comforter to hold the layers together.

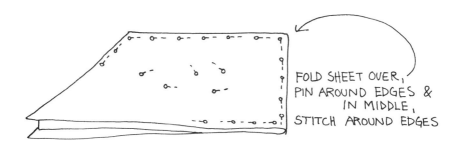

Sew around all four sides of the comforter about ½ inch (1 cm.) or more from the edge, stitching through all three layers. It's best to do this with a sewing machine so the stitching will be very firm. Then sew through the comforter in a simple design to hold the layers together. You could make a series of rectangles about 6 inches (15 cm.) inside one another, or straight lines from corner to corner or across in one direction. This completes your comforter.

Matching Dust Ruffle

What You'll Need:
1 flat sheet or other fabric
1 old contour sheet
sewing machine or needle and thread

Of course, you can make a dust ruffle for your bed out of almost any material and then just tuck in your blanket all the way around for a finished look to your bed. But if you've made a comforter you'll probably want to make a dust ruffle to match. It doesn't have to be made of exactly the same material; you could use a plain fabric that goes with the colors in your comforter. But it's easy to get another sheet when you buy the one for your comforter and then make a matched set.

The easiest kind of dust ruffle to make isn't really ruffled. It gives a tailored or sporty look and would look great in a striped or plaid sheet fabric. It could also be made from other fabric, such as corduroy, denim, burlap, or quilted cotton, that matches or contrasts with your comforter.

You'll need a contour sheet that fits your bed. It can be an old, torn one of any color or pattern, as long as the edges are still more or less intact.

Measure from the top of your box springs to the floor; this distance will probably be from 12 to 15 inches (30–38 cm.). Then measure the length and width of the box springs. You will need two strips of fabric the length of the box springs plus 2 inches (5 cm.) and one strip the width of the box springs plus 2 inches (5 cm.). All three strips should be as wide as the distance from the floor to the top of the box springs. When you cut the strips, measure from the selvage edge of the fabric for each one so you can use the selvage edge at the bottom of the dust ruffle—then you won't need to hem. If you're using a sheet, cut the short strip from the bottom end of the sheet so you can use the small hem, and cut the long strips from the sides of the sheet. Save the fabric you don't use for other decorative touches in your room. If you have enough left over, you might want to make a pillow for your bed or the floor (see page 88).

Take your mattress off the bed and put the contour sheet on the box springs. Pull it smooth so the edges are down as far as

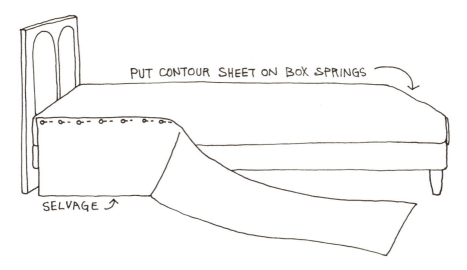

possible. Now pin the cut edges of the strips to the sheet so the selvage edges just clear the floor. Start pinning at the head of the bed, bringing the strip around the corner about 1 inch (2½ cm.). At the bottom corners the strips will overlap a little; you can turn the edges under a bit if you like.

When the strips are all pinned and hang evenly, sew them to the sheet. Use a machine, or use doubled thread and medium-size running stitches. You can probably sew it by hand while it's still on the bed. Take all the pins out and you're finished!

A ruffly dust ruffle is much more difficult to make. Before you buy the material to make one, check the bedding departments of department and discount stores. Although most ready-made bedspreads and dust ruffles are quite expensive, there are plain colored cotton dust ruffles available that don't cost a whole lot more than the material you'll have to buy if you make one. Be sure to look during sales. You might find what you want at a price you can afford.

If you really want to make a ruffly dust ruffle, you will need twice as much fabric and also a good deal more time than you needed for a tailored one. Use lightweight cotton—sheets are fine. If you use a sheet, first cut off the wide top hem. Then measure up from each selvage edge the distance from the top of your box springs to the floor plus 2 inches (5 cm.). Cut these two strips straight. Then measure this same distance from these cut edges and cut two more straight strips. You'll probably end up with a little strip left over in the center of the sheet. Now

make two parallel lines of machine stitching using a long stitch, or medium-size running stitches near the top edge of each of the four strips. Measure the distance around the two sides and

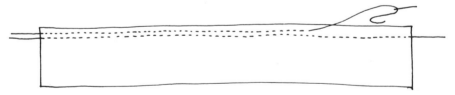

foot of the box springs. Divide this distance by 4. Gather each strip by carefully pulling the two top threads if you have machine stitching, or the two threads of hand stitching. When the gathered edge of each strip is one fourth the whole distance around the box springs, tie knots in the threads to secure them. Then sew a line of machine stitching or firm running stitches

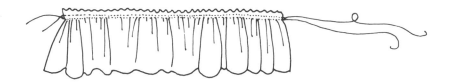

across the gathers to hold them in place. When all four strips are gathered, pin and sew them to the contour sheet. Overlap the ends of the strips where they meet, and make sure that the bottom edges hang straight just off the floor.

☆slapdash tip

If You Don't Have Box Springs

What do you do if your bed doesn't have box springs? You can still make a dust ruffle for it. Use an old sheet or piece of fabric that's just a little bigger than the bed frame for the base. Lay this fabric on top of the bed frame or springs so that a little material drapes over the edges and the end. Then follow the directions for making your own dust ruffle (page 77), attaching the ruffle to the fabric base instead of to a contour sheet.

Quilted Bedspread

What You'll Need:
2 flat sheets (your bed size)
polyester batting
sewing machine

You can make a whole quilted bedspread the same way you make a comforter. Of course, you'll want only one layer of batting so the bedspread will lie flat. You could use already quilted material to make the bedspread (see page 74), but if you use sheets you will be able to match your bedspread to curtains or a night-table cover or other things in your room. You could even use plain sheets and design them with fabric spray paint.

Lay the batting flat on the floor and then lay one sheet flat on top of it. Cut the batting about ½ inch (1 cm.) smaller than the sheet all the way around. Then lay one sheet flat on the

floor wrong side up, spread the the batting evenly on top of it, and then put the other sheet on top right side up. Pin around all four edges and sew through all three layers. Because the edges of the sheets are finished, you don't have to hem them or turn them under. Instead of quilting in straight lines or rectangles, why not draw a design on the quilt that follows the design of the sheet? Then sew through the quilt along the lines you've drawn for a really handsome quilted bedspread.

Floors

Floors are difficult and expensive to change. New floor coverings, whether carpet, tile, or linoleum, require professional installation. Refinishing wood floors is a major undertaking and is extremely difficult to do well. So what you've got is pretty much what you'll have to live with. However, there are a number of ways you can create small or medium-size rugs that will change the whole look of your room. You can also make comfortable floor pillows to make your room a great place for friends to gather.

In many cities you can find carpet remnant stores, and large carpet stores sometimes have remnant sections. These are great sources of bargains. Look for carpet pad remnants there too.

Jazzing Up a Room-size Rug

What You'll Need:
old rug
rug remnants for border
utility knife
carpet tape

If you have an old rug for your room that's a little smaller than you'd like or is just boring, you can liven it up with a border made from carpet remnants. This is also a good solution for a rug that's frayed and tattered around the edges.

First shop around to see what's available. Look in second-hand stores for pieces of still good carpet at a bargain. You will probably want carpet remnants that are about the same thickness as your original rug. But have you considered a fluffy white border for a dark or tweedy flat rug? As long as you're making changes, think about doing something really dramatic!

When you buy carpet remnants to attach to your rug, make sure you have measured what you want correctly and keep in mind that a few large pieces will be easier to attach than a lot of small ones. In fact, you may find one big piece of carpet that can be cut into four strips to make a border all the way around your rug. Or how about making a series of different colored stripes at the ends of your rug?

You will attach the border pieces to the center rug by taping the edges of rug together at the back. Ask at a carpet store, large hardware store, or building supply store for tape to do this job. You need very strong tape that's about 4 inches (10 cm.) wide. Don't try to use iron-on carpet tape, though; it's difficult to apply and you can easily ruin the iron and burn yourself.

If you decide to cut down your original rug before adding a border, be sure to ask first whether this is all right. If so, mark the back of the rug and use a utility knife to cut it. Do all cutting on a *thick* layer of newspaper (outdoors if possible) and be *very careful*. Measure and cut the border pieces carefully with the utility knife to make them all fit neatly. Then turn all the pieces over and tape the backs of the border remnants to the back of the center rug and to each other.

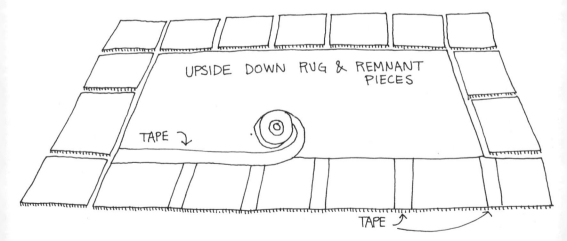

Safari Rug

What You'll Need:
fake fur
carpet pad
fabric glue

Here's a way to make a conservation-minded tiger skin rug that will feel warm and toasty on your feet on winter mornings. Get a carpet pad remnant (not the rubber kind) the size of the rug you want. Then buy fake fur fabric the same size. Use fabric glue (available in hardware and building supply stores) to attach the fur to the top surface of the carpet pad. Work carefully to be sure the fur is smooth and flat. The carpet pad will give the rug body and keep it from sliding around.

Patchwork Area Rug

What You'll Need:
carpet samples or remnants
carpet pad
fabric glue

You can use several small rug remnants or rug samples to make your own patchwork rug. Arrange them on a piece of carpet pad (not the rubber kind) in a design that appeals to you. When you're happy with it, attach the patches to the carpet pad the same way you attached the fake fur (above). Make sure the patchwork pieces meet at all the edges so there aren't any gaps.

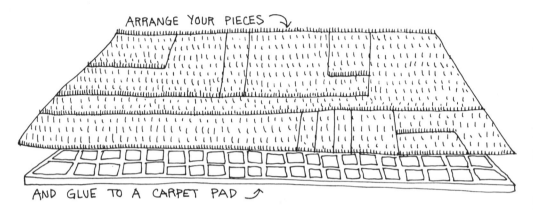

Floor Pillows

What You'll Need:
fabric
stuffing—shredded polyurethane foam or foam squares
needle and thread
optional: snaps or Velcro dots

A collection of colorful floor pillows is like comfortable furniture that can be moved wherever you want it. If you have a variety of shapes and sizes, you and your friends will always have something just right to curl up on.

In choosing fabrics for floor pillows, you can let your imagination roam free. Amazingly enough, the strangest and most diverse patterns and color combinations seem to blend harmoniously when you have a bunch of pillows. Pieces from old brocade curtains look great next to Indian prints or bright graphics. And, of course, this is a great way to use leftover fabric from other projects. Corduroy, velour, and velveteen can be mixed with cotton prints or gingham checks. You can even use two different fabrics in one pillow. Just make sure the fabrics you use are tightly woven, so the stuffing won't leak through, and are not too scratchy to sit or lie on.

The simplest kind of pillow is made from two equal squares or rectangles of fabric. Lay the pieces with right sides together and pin along three edges. Then sew by machine or with firm hand stitching about ½ inch (1 cm.) from these edges. Turn the pillow cover right side out and stuff it with shredded foam rubber or polyurethane. Shredded foam as well as foam squares can be found in fabric, building supply, and department stores, or in some dime stores. This is a messy job because the bits of foam cling like mad to everything. So wear old clothes and work outside or on a linoleum floor.

PIN & STITCH THREE SIDES

TURN INSIDE OUT & STUFF YOUR PILLOW

Some of your pillows can be full and firm while others are squishy. When the pillow is as full as you want it, pin the top edges together, turning under ½ inch (1 cm.) or so of each edge. Sew by machine or by hand close to the edge.

Try making other shapes like triangles, hexagons, circles, or even free-form shapes. Just make sure you leave a big enough opening to stuff through.

You can also make a new removable

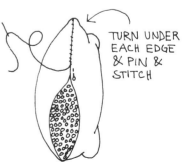
TURN UNDER EACH EDGE & PIN & STITCH

cover for an old floor pillow. Make it the same way as the pillow cover above. Push the pillow inside it. Sew individual snaps or snap tape on both inner edges for a neat closing, or use Velcro tape or dots. If you use washable fabric, you can take the cover off and wash it whenever you have to.

You can also make firm solid pillows by covering thick foam rubber squares. You need a piece of fabric about 6 inches (15 cm.) wider than the foam square and about 2 inches (5 cm.) longer than the distance all the way around the square. Wrap the fabric wrong side out around the pillow form; pull it smooth and pin the ends together in a straight line to form a tube with open sides. Don't make the fabric too tight around the pillow—leave it slightly loose. Then slide the fabric off the pillow and sew the ends together along the line of pins.

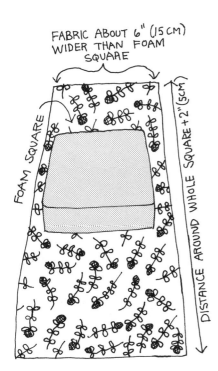

Turn the fabric right side out and push the pillow into the tube, leaving equal amounts of fabric at the two open sides. Fold up this fabric neatly on each side as if you were wrapping a package. Turn the raw edge under at each side and sew it down by hand.

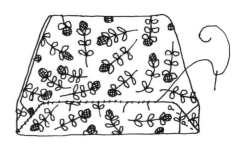

☆slapdash tip

Soften Up Your Study Chair!

Where else do you sit besides on the floor? Cushion your desk chair with a flat foam rubber pad cut to fit the seat. Choose fabric coordinated with your bedspread or curtains and cover the pad as above. Ribbon ties sewed to the back corners will keep it on the chair. To be really comfortable, make another cushion for the chair back; sew ties to all four corners to keep it in place.

Walls

When you've got your furniture and big things like curtains and bedspread installed, you'll probably want to put something on the walls to complete your décor.

The projects in this chapter are intended to enhance the walls of your room, but not to make drastic permanent changes in them. Painting walls, wallpapering, and major carpentry are not slapdash projects; they are difficult and time-consuming, and unless they are done just right they look terrible. So if you plan to try any of these, ask a professional for advice and help.

But don't despair! Even without major surgery, your room can look dramatically different with a few creative changes in your wall decoration.

Hangings

What You'll Need:
fabric
2 wooden dowels
cord
pushpin or thumbtack
needle and thread

The easiest kind of wall hanging is a rectangle of fabric. Look in old trunks and in thrift shops—you may find a fantastic piece of antique or imported fabric that will transform your room. It doesn't have to be in perfect condition as long as the over-all look is right.

You'll need two dowels (slim round

lightweight rods that are cheap and easy to find at hardware stores or lumberyards) and a decorative cord or ribbon. The dowels should be about 4 inches (10 cm.) longer than the width of the fabric, and the cord must be a little longer than one dowel. Turn the fabric under at the top and bottom and sew straight across to make casings wide enough to slip the dowels through. Just make sure the top and bottom edges of the fabric are folded straight or it will hang crooked. Slip the dowels through the casings so that an even amount of wood sticks out on each side. Tie the ends of the cord around the top dowel at both edges of the fabric for hanging.

Your fabric wall hanging will probably be very lightweight and could be hung from a pushpin or thumbtack in the wall.

Illusion Bed Canopy

What You'll Need:
patterned sheet or other large
   piece of fabric
decorative lightweight curtain rod
2 large picture hooks
narrow ribbon or cord

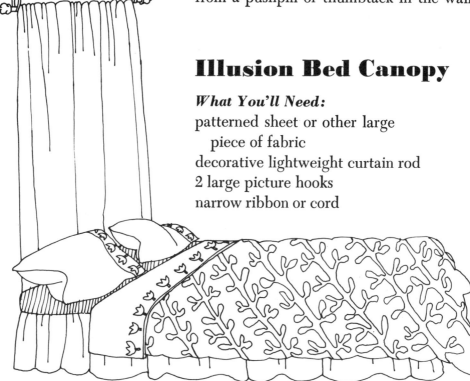

Wouldn't you love to have a canopy over your bed? Of course a real canopy is expensive and hard to build, but you can create a similar softening look with an illusion canopy. For a modern-looking room with clean, simple lines, use a bold abstract or scenic print. If your room has a more delicate décor, try fabric that has a muted watercolor look. Of course, you can also use a patterned sheet that matches your comforter or dust ruffle.

You need fabric about as long as the distance from floor to ceiling. Cut it to the width of your bed for a flat hanging, or use a wider piece (like a whole sheet) for a fuller, softer effect.

Buy a decorative curtain rod with fancy end knobs; it should be as long as the width of your bed. If you're using a sheet, you won't need to make a casing; just slide the rod through the wide hem at the top of the sheet, and bunch up the fabric to make the canopy the same width as your bed. For other pieces of fabric, turn one end under and sew it to make a casing that's wide enough for the rod to slide through.

Now nail in the picture hooks at the very top of the wall, directly above the corners of your bed. Hang the rod from the picture hooks with loops of ribbon or cord. Make the loops as long as you like; just be sure they are both the same length. If the fabric drags on the floor when it's hung, cut off or hem the bottom edge so it clears the floor behind the head of your bed.

For That Romantic Look

A billowy curtain canopy may be just the right romantic touch for your room. Make your canopy out of lightweight fabric that's a good deal wider than your bed; try a lovely flowered sheet one size larger than your bed takes. Cut it in half lengthwise and hang the two pieces as above. Tie a wide velvet ribbon in a big bow around each half of the canopy and thumbtack the bows to the wall at the outer edges of the canopy so it will hang open.

Posters

What You'll Need:
posters
pushpins or thumbtacks
spray plastic or polyurethane
optional: art board, glue, stick-on picture hanger

Depending on the décor of your room, a collection of big splashy posters could look terrific. Tack them right on the wall with pushpins or thumbtacks. Spray them with plastic or polyurethane before you put them up to protect them.

If you'd prefer to mount your posters, there's an easy way to do it. A sheet of art board a little larger than your poster makes both the backing and the "frame." Art board comes in a huge selection of colors and is available in art supply stores. Take your poster with you and pick out a color that will complement it.

Use a yardstick and pencil to center your poster on the artboard. When you've marked the position of the poster on the board, spread rubber cement or white glue evenly across the top back edge of the poster. Make sure to bring the glue all the way out to the corners and edges of the poster. Then glue the top of the poster carefully in place on the board. When the top is in position, spread glue on the side edges of the back of the poster, smoothing the poster in place as you go from top to bottom. Put a strip of glue across the bottom back the same way you did the top.

When your poster is dry, attach a stick-on picture hanger to the back of the art board. (Follow package directions.) Put it 2 to 3 inches (5–7½ cm.) down from the top and make sure it is exactly centered or the poster won't hang straight. Now attach another stick-on picture hanger to the wall where you'd like your poster to hang. Be sure to wait at least half an hour for the hangers to dry before hanging one from the other.

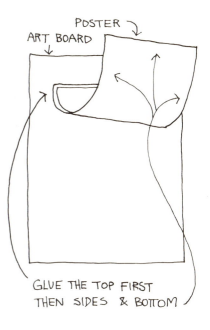

GLUE THE TOP FIRST THEN SIDES & BOTTOM

Do-it-yourself "Wallpaper"

What You'll Need:
posters (or other decorative items)
pushpins or thumbtacks

How about "wallpapering" one entire wall from floor to ceiling with a combination of movie posters, or travel posters and a giant map? What a great way to remember a trip or special event. Did you know that you can get beautiful *free* posters from the tourist bureaus of most foreign countries? Look in the phone book or ask a travel agent where to write.

Or how would you like a sports wall with a collection of action shots and photos of sports stars punctuated with scorecards, pennants, and advertising posters? You can "wallpaper" your wall with almost anything that's flat. Make a "crazy quilt" out of wallpaper samples or old calendar pictures. Or turn your wall into a photo gallery with all those great pictures of family and friends pinned to make a solid wall of photos. Use thumbtacks or pushpins to put up your "wallpaper" and then you can change it when you get another inspiration.

Framing Pictures

What You'll Need:
old picture frame
paint
art board
optional: cardboard, finishing nails, wire, screw eyes

Picture frames tend to be very expensive. You might be able to find inexpensive frames for small pictures in a five-and-ten, but frames for large or irregular-size pictures almost always cost a lot of money. Look in secondhand stores and thrift shops for bargains in old picture frames you can repaint. If a frame still has a picture in it, all you need to do is take the backing off. Use pliers to pull out the tiny finishing nails that hold the backing in the frame (be sure to save the nails). Then remove the various layers until you get to the picture. Take out the old picture and put yours in. If you want or need a mat around your picture and can't find one pre-cut, glue your picture to a piece of colored art board cut to fit the frame. Do this the same way you did for a poster (page 96) before putting it in the frame. (It's tricky to cut your own mats straight.) Then replace the layers the way you found them, and push the finishing nails firmly back into their holes.

If all you've got is a frame with nothing in it, cut a piece of art board to fit snugly inside the frame. Center your picture and glue it to the art board. Put this inside the frame and then put a piece of corrugated cardboard (cut to the same size) behind it. Hammer a few finishing nails sideways into the inside back edge of the frame to hold the picture securely. Even without glass, a frame will give your picture a more important and finished look. For a hanging wire, put a screw eye into the back of the frame about one third of the way down from the top on either side. Run a piece of wire across the back through the screw eyes and twist the ends to hold.

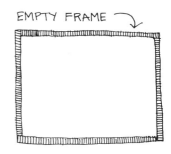

EMPTY FRAME

ART BOARD WITH PICTURE

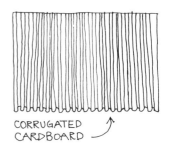

CORRUGATED CARDBOARD

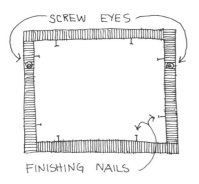

SCREW EYES

FINISHING NAILS

HANGING PICTURES

The terrific part about stick-on picture hangers is that you don't have to make a hole in your wall with a nail, and you can take them off the wall quite easily without leaving a mark by using a damp cloth. (Keep applying the cloth gently to the hanger until it comes off the wall by itself.) However, heavier things like mirrors need the stronger support of regular picture hooks. And if you're hanging pictures in the bathroom, you can't use stick-on hooks because the steam will make them slide right off the wall. When you nail regular picture hooks into the wall, put a short strip of masking tape on the wall first and hammer the nail through it. This will help keep paint and plaster from chipping off, but a little paint will probably come off with the masking tape if you ever remove it.

All in all, pushpins and thumbtacks are the least damaging to walls but can be used to hold up only very light items. Stick-on picture hangers are a terrific way of hanging things on the walls without making holes but they won't work for very heavy things or in steamy areas. Use regular picture hooks as a last resort and be sure you know where you want them before you start pounding them into the walls!

STICK-ON HANGER

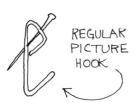
REGULAR PICTURE HOOK

PUSHPIN

THUMBTACK

100

Bulletin Board

What You'll Need:
Celotex *or* sheet of corrugated cardboard and felt to cover it
mirror clips or other hardware
paint or other decorative material

A bulletin board is a great spot to display a changing collection of pictures as well as reminders to yourself, postcards, and photographs. It's so easy to put stuff on and take it off that you can even change your display to match the seasons. Souvenirs from camp or parties, athletic letters and awards, and your favorite (lightweight) doodads make your bulletin board a very personal scrapbook.

A giant bulletin board is not hard to make. Buy Celotex, a material about ½ inch (1 cm.) thick that comes in large sheets about 4 by 8 feet (1 × 2½ meters). It is inexpensive and is available at discount building supply stores. Use a whole sheet or have it cut to the size you want. You can paint it or cover it with fabric if you like. Attach it vertically or horizontally to your wall with mirror clips, nails, or other hardware. Ask the building supply salesperson what is best for your walls.

If you want a border for your bulletin board, pin fancy embroidered tape, fringe, or bobbles from the notions counter to the edges. Or glue shells, artificial flowers, or fancy bows from presents to make a unique border.

☆ slapdash tip
Glitter Glamour

Why not personalize your bulletin board—write your name in glitter at the top! Use white glue to write the letters and then shake glitter over the wet glue. (Use lots of newspaper—this is a messy project!) Or you can use glitter to make a border all around the board.

Another way to make your own bulletin board is to cut a sheet of corrugated cardboard to the size you want. To dress it up, and to make the tacks hold better, glue felt over the whole bulletin board; use a color that goes well with your room.

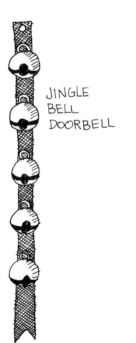

JINGLE BELL DOORBELL

☆ slapdash tip
Make a Ribbon Display!

Do you have a collection of bizarre pin-on buttons like the ones used in political campaigns? Get a long piece of wide ribbon and pin the buttons to it. Tack the top end of the ribbon to your wall with pushpins or thumbtacks for display. You can do the same thing with snapshots or school pictures of your friends. Pin the pictures to the ribbon with straight pins. How about tacking one or two ribbon displays to the door of your room? You could even sew jingle bells to a ribbon and tack it to the outside of the door for your own private doorbell!

Wall Headboard

What You'll Need:
piece of carpet
6 nails

If your bed doesn't have a headboard, you can make yourself a comfortable back rest that will be a spectacular addition to your room. You need a piece of carpet as wide as your bed and long enough to cover the wall from floor to ceiling. Check to see if your family has clean leftover carpet you can use, or look in discount carpet stores for a remnant that would be just right for your room.

Cut the carpet to the right size with a utility knife; work on several layers of newspaper and go carefully! Then attach the carpet with four nails at the top and one at each bottom corner (make sure no one objects before you start hammering).

This ultra-dramatic effect will be the main focal point of your room, so do it first and then see what other wall hangings will complement it.

Accessories

Accessories are the smaller decorative or useful items that pull your décor together and make the room function really well. These are the finishing touches that make the room uniquely yours.

What you choose as accessories for your room depends largely on what else you've done in the way of fabrics, colors, patterns, and textures for the big areas. And it especially depends on what you plan to do in your room. You may have a room full of dainty pastels and delicate fabrics which would look pretty weird with a bold graphic poster slapped on the wall. And if your room has an American Indian motif you won't want frilly lampshades or ornate picture frames. Instead, use baskets for plants, pencils, and wastebaskets, and Indian-looking pottery dishes for paper clips or hairpins. Put burlap or other natural-looking fabric on lampshades.

As you search for accessories, you will probably find yourself drawn to things that go together; this is not too surprising, since you are the one who chose the look for your room to begin with. Just remember to consider not only how you will use a certain accessory but also how it will look in your room.

It's a big temptation to cover every inch of wall and surface space with little treasures. But this can give your room a cluttered, junky look. You don't need to be really spartan, but it is best to start with only a few things you know you'll like or need. Then you can add new things slowly as you come across the perfect item for each spot.

FIXING UP OLD LAMPS AND LAMPSHADES
Good lighting is important in any room. Start by thinking about where you'll need lamps. Do you always flop on your bed to study or curl up on floor pillows in a corner? Or do you sit at

your desk most of the time? You'll need a good reading lamp to study by as well as a light on your vanity or on your bedside table.

New lamps are expensive, but you might be able to find a couple of old floor or table lamps that aren't being used. If the wiring is in good shape, you can probably make these old lamps look terrific.

If the base looks pretty crummy, paint it. For a metal lamp base, use spray paint that is especially for use on metal. Get it at a hardware or paint store and be sure to cover everything with newspaper before you start spraying.

If you want to buy a new lampshade, you can find inexpensive shades in five-and-tens or discount stores. Or maybe a Japanese lantern-type shade from an import store would look nice. But it's more fun to create your own. If you like the shape of the original shade, cover it with fabric or patterned paper. Tape a piece of newspaper around the shade and trim it to fit the lampshade; this will be your pattern. Use the pattern to cut the paper or fabric to the size you need, allowing about ½-inch (1-cm.) overlap. For a cone-shaped shade, you might find it easier to cut the fabric in two or three pieces to get a better fit.

Test the new shade cover against the old shade to make sure the size is right. Next, spread white glue thinly all over the

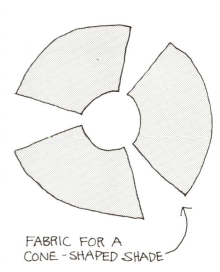

FABRIC FOR A CONE-SHAPED SHADE

shade, and then glue the new fabric or paper carefully to the shade, smoothing it with your fingers.

Another possibility is to glue magazine or other cut-out pictures onto the old shade for a collage. Before you glue them down, test to see whether the writing on the back of the pictures shows through when the lamp is lighted. If it does, use a layer of plain paper under the collage.

Light a Matching Lamp!

Make your lampshade an integral part of your decorating scheme! It will look as if it's been made especially for you when you cover it with the same fabric you've used elsewhere in your room. If patterned sheets are used in your décor, some of that fabric would be perfect.

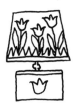

Making a Lamp

What You'll Need:
stick-in corked lamp socket and cord
bottle for base
shade
decorative trim, colored sand, or other decorative material

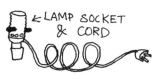

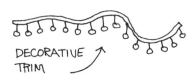

In a hardware store you can buy a light socket and cord for making a lamp. This whole unit is already put together; all you need is a lamp base and a shade. The socket generally has a narrow cork bottom that fits into the neck of a wine bottle or narrow-necked ceramic vase. A wine bottle makes a good base because it is fairly stable. You can make it even steadier by partially filling it with sand or fine gravel.

If the bottle has a woven straw basket around it, you won't even need to decorate it. But if it's plain glass, you can decorate it with paint (get the kind that works on glass) or a glued-on collage. You could gather together a bunch of your favorite sports pictures and use them as the collage to make a super sports lamp. Or what about gluing stripes or spirals of notions trim such as rickrack, embroidered or metallic ribbon, lace, or even fringe? Look in your box of odds and ends for crazy combinations.

Get an inexpensive plain clip-on shade and decorate it the same way as the lamp base. A frilly feminine lamp can be an eye-catcher on a vanity; a lamp covered with photos of your family or favorite sports stars would make studying at your desk more fun.

If you have a large clear glass bottle, consider how it would look as a lamp. You could fill it with different-colored

PARTIALLY FILL WITH SAND OR FINE GRAVEL

A STICK IS USED TO CREATE THE DESIGNS

A CLEAR GLASS BOTTLE CAN BE FILLED WITH SAND OF DIFFERENT COLORS

layers of sand for a super sand picture. (Get colored sand at a hobby shop.) After each layer is added, use a long thin stick or wire to push the new color down around the edges to form the design. Just be careful not to stir the sand too much, or the colors will run together.

CONTAINERS
Somehow everyone seems to need a number of containers to keep stuff in. Some of the best containers are "found" or converted from other uses. Gifts often come in fancy boxes or jars that would be just right for your card games or bobby pins. So don't throw out the packaging without thinking over what you might use it for. Another source of free containers is the kitchen; cans of all sizes and various shaped jars can be rescued from the trash, decorated, and used to hold desk supplies or odds and ends.

If you buy containers, check in discount import shops and large hardware stores; they carry a wide selection of inexpensive jars, bottles, baskets, and boxes.

Wastebaskets

What You'll Need:
square of wood, 4 sticks, caning, and staple gun
or cardboard container
or old wastebasket
paint and other decorations

No room is complete without a wastebasket, but these are often unattractive or boring. With a little ingenuity you can create a wastebasket that won't have to be hidden under the desk. A wicker basket can be a decorative accent, especially if you use other baskets in your room. You can find quite inexpensive baskets in shapes that will work well at shops that sell accessories for house plants and in the housewares department of some large department stores. You might get two and put a potted floor plant in the other one.

You can even make your own basket-style wastebasket. Get a piece of wood (pressed wood or plywood is fine) from the lumberyard. You need a square or rectangle that will be the right size for the bottom of your wastebasket, and you might find what you want in the scrap barrel in the lumberyard. You also need four small pieces of wood or sticks to go around the top of the wastebasket. Look for these in the scrap bin too. Buy enough caning (at a building supply or hardware or craft store) to go around the outside edge of the wood square. With a staple gun, staple one edge of the caning around the outside edge of the wood base, letting the ends of the caning overlap a little. Glue or staple the ends of caning together where they overlap. Then put the strips of wood inside the top edges of the caning so they form a top of the basket the same size and shape as the bottom base. Glue or staple the caning to the wood pieces and you're finished.

A plain sturdy cardboard box can look very jazzy as a wastebasket if you cover it with contact paper, wallpaper remnants, or fabric. Even better is a large round

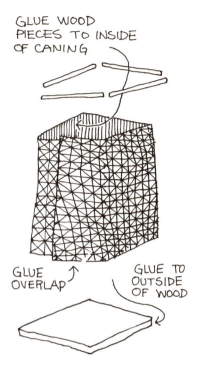

cardboard ice-cream container. Maybe your local soda fountain or ice-cream shop will give you an empty 5- or 10-gallon drum. This is very sturdy and it looks great when it's painted or decorated with a collage of colorful paper and/or fabric scraps.

Burlap is a good fabric for covering cardboard containers, because the cardboard color looks natural showing through. Just cut the covering 1 inch (2½ cm.) or so longer than the box in both directions. Put a thin layer of glue all over the box. Overlap the edges of the covering where they meet and glue the top edge over the edge of the box.

Even an ugly old wastebasket gets a new lease on life when it's refurbished with fabric, paper, or paint. You could glue on fabric to match your bedspread or curtains, or plain fabric stenciled with fabric paint. Or glue leftover wallpaper to the wastebasket. If your decorating scheme carries into a bathroom, do the same to the wastebasket there for a co-ordinated look.

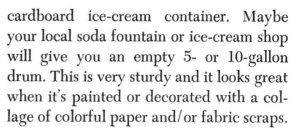

How About a Hamper?

Don't throw your dirty clothes in the bottom of your closet or kick them into a corner! Make a hamper one of your room's accessories. A decorated cardboard carton or a big basket works fine. But why not be really different and use a clean small-size garbage can (plastic or metal)? And when you've got it, flaunt it—paint it all over with street signs like "No Parking," "One Way," "Towaway Zone," and "STOP"!

Desk-top Accessories

What You'll Need:
a variety of containers
paint and other decorative materials

Is the top of your desk cluttered with pencils, paper clips, and other loose but necessary items? Wouldn't it be convenient to have all your pencils and pens in one spot so you don't have to search through your drawers to find one? The answer is to organize! And you can do it decoratively. Make a matched set of containers to hold writing tools, paper clips, rubber bands, letters and notes, and anything else you need.

Collect empty cans of useful sizes—a tuna fish can is great for small clips or tacks, a medium-tall can holds a ruler and letter opener as well as pencils, and a wider fruit or vegetable can will keep all your unanswered letters and small papers together. Be sure the cans have been

opened cleanly so there are no jagged edges to cut you. Remove the labels and wash and dry the cans before you start.

Now's the time to take a creative look at all your odds and ends of decorating materials. Do you have fabric or contact paper left over from another project? Or what about recycling some gorgeous gift-wrapping paper for an eye-catching container set? Choose any paper or fabric that goes with the rest of your room and glue it on the cans.

For a room that has bold graphics everywhere, you could paint your cans with bands of color, using paint that's made for metal. Or you can cover the desk container set with collages of pictures or scraps of paper and fabric. You can wrap the cans with plain or braided yarn or string; smear glue in a thin layer all over the can and wind the yarn around it, keeping the rows close together. Or label the cans with colored tape on the shiny metal surface.

Another unusual kind of container for your desk set is a group of clay flowerpots. These are sold inexpensively in hardware stores and plant shops. It's better to buy new ones so they will be clean. They come in all sizes from tiny to gigantic! Get whatever sizes you need and don't forget a little clay saucer for paper clips and other small objects. The terracotta clay is quite attractive all by itself so you really don't need

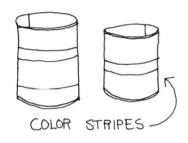

COLOR STRIPES

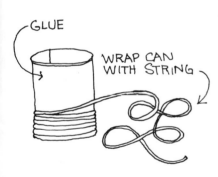

GLUE

WRAP CAN WITH STRING

112

to decorate this set. Just tape over the drainage hole in the bottom of each pot so nothing will fall through.

Lots of other household items go together to make a useful collection of desk accessories. A striking mug is just the right size for pencils and pens and rulers. Plain glass coasters (you can get the kind that go under the legs of furniture at hardware stores) hold paper clips and rubber bands. And a medium-sized basket is an attractive catch-all for letters and other papers. Even an old Easter basket would look great, repainted with spray paint. Keep your eyes open for other possibilities that might be just what you need on your desk.

Vanity-top Accessories

What You'll Need:
a variety of containers
decorative materials

Vanities, too, usually need a bunch of containers to hold all those doodads. Of course, you could use the same kinds of things you used for your desk, but you might want something a little fancier. Plain or patterned glass containers look dainty and elegant. You may discover some treasures around the house that you can

TERRACOTTA CLAY POTS

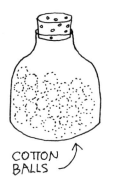

COTTON BALLS

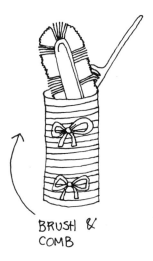

BRUSH & COMB

put to use. Maybe someone's given you a short fat jar of homemade jam with a pretty patterned lid. When the jam's gone that glass jar would make a great holder for hairpins or safety pins. In fact, many presents come in attractive glass containers, like bell jars full of candy. A big one is great for holding cotton balls or scented soap. Or how about sticking rollers in it and tying a fat ribbon around the outside of the jar in a bow? You can even buy new glass containers cheaply at five-and-tens and hardware stores.

ROLLERS

You can use pretty china or pottery bowls for hairbands and all those other odds and ends. Stand up brushes (handle down) and combs in a tallish container that isn't too fragile. You could cover this container by gluing on strips of colored ribbons. Leave the ends of one or two ribbons long to tie in a bow.

Another handy item is a small tray to hold all your bottles and jars. If you find one around the house, don't worry if it's rather beat-up. Let yourself go in redecorating it. Sequins, glitter, beads, or shells glued around the edges might make a glamorous finishing touch. Then you could glue this same trim around the frame of an inexpensive mirror to hang over your vanity.

MIRROR WITH SHELLS & RIBBON DECORATION

Dresser Accessories

What You'll Need:
a variety of containers
decorative materials
optional: tray

Boys seem to collect as much stuff on the tops of their dressers as girls. A big metal or ceramic stein holds a brush, combs, and a shoehorn. An inexpensive or beat-up old tray is great to keep together all that stuff that accumulates. You can probably buy a cheap small plastic or pressed wood tray at the five-and-ten. How about covering it with a collage of cartoons and exciting or funny headlines clipped from newspapers or magazines? Just glue them on firmly and spray the whole tray with plastic after the glue dries.

A box with a lid is useful on top of a dresser. It can hold jewelry or coins or other treasures. Cigar boxes are fairly

CIGAR BOXES ARE VERY USEFUL

easy to get. Ask the tobacconist to save you one when it's empty. If you like the design on it you can use it just as it is. Otherwise decorate it any way you like.

Sometimes other things, like fancy soaps, come in hinged wooden boxes. They're terrific for jewelry and you may not even want to decorate the outside. But you can easily make a velveteen liner for the inside that will protect your jewelry. Cut shirt cardboard or the back of a writing pad into five pieces just a little bit smaller than the bottom and four sides of the box's interior. Cut pieces of velveteen a little larger all around than each piece of cardboard. Smooth the velveteen over one side of a cardboard piece and wrap the extra fabric over all the edges. Hold it down on the back with masking tape. Do the same with the other four pieces. Then push the bottom piece into the box first so it lies flat. Now slide in the side pieces. The tight fit will keep the liner in place. If it gaps at the top, use double-stick tape to hold it. You can also line the lid if you want.

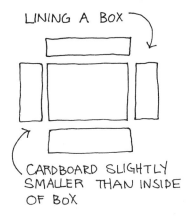

LINING A BOX

CARDBOARD SLIGHTLY SMALLER THAN INSIDE OF BOX

VELVETEEN
CARDBOARD
MASKING TAPE

Drawer Organizers

What You'll Need:
a variety of cardboard boxes
a cupcake tin or a kitchen utensil tray
optional: decorative materials

What a treat to have dividers in your dresser or desk drawers to keep everything neatly in place! It's very difficult to make real dividers that attach to the drawers. Instead, try using cardboard boxes for a quick and easy set of compartments for all your odds and ends. Gather boxes of the various sizes you need. Shoe boxes, shirt and sweater boxes, jewelry boxes, and all those odd-sized boxes that gifts come in should give you plenty of variety. Christmas card and stationery boxes are especially good. Don't worry if some of the boxes are too tall for your drawers. You can cut the sides down to make them fit. If you like, you can use fun fabrics to line the boxes the same way you lined the jewelry box (page 116).

Why not use an old cupcake tin (look in a thrift shop) or a kitchen silverware holder in your top drawer to hold coins, old marbles, cufflinks, achievement medals, and other small but heavy items? These are useful for desk drawers too, to keep anything from pencils to pushpins sorted out and easily visible. Spray-paint it in some exotic color (use paint made for metal). Small pieces of jewelry can be kept in see-through plastic boxes

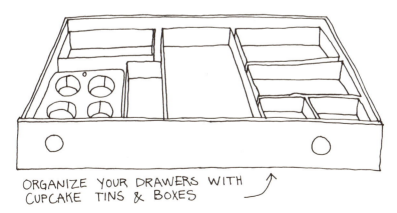

ORGANIZE YOUR DRAWERS WITH CUPCAKE TINS & BOXES

with compartments (the kind sold in hardware and dime stores for nails and tacks), so you can find what you want in an instant.

PLANTS AND LIVING THINGS

Just like fresh air and sunshine, plants are great to have in your room. They add color and texture and it's a lot of fun to take care of them and watch them grow. Some (especially flowering plants) need direct sunlight. Many others (like philodendron, grape ivy, wandering Jew, spider plants, and even begonias and African violets) need only indirect light. But there aren't any green, leafy plants that do well in a very dark corner! So the light source is an important consideration in deciding what kind of plants you can keep and where to put them. Some plants are very easy to grow and others are not. The place where you get your plants or a good reference book will tell you what you need to know about taking care of the kinds you select.

Of course, you can line up your potted plants on your windowsill or on the floor under your window. And you can make bracketed shelves across your window (page 53) to put plants on. But have you thought about using a sturdy potted plant as a bookend in your bookcase? Or how about on the corner of your desk? Consider putting small plants in pretty pots on your dresser or vanity. And, of course, you can hang trailing plants from the ceiling or the top of the window frame to make a curtain of greenery. Just make sure the hooks or brackets you hang them from are sturdy enough to support their weight.

☆slapdash tip

Two Points for Plants!

If hanging plants from the top of your window frame keeps your curtains from closing, here's an inventive way to solve the problem. Attach a basketball hoop (spray-paint it first if you like) with screws or molly bolts to the window frame or wall. Then hang your pots at different levels from the hoop. The hoop sticks out far enough so you can easily close your curtains and you'll have a whole jungle of plants you can see day or night!

Most plants come in ugly plastic containers. If the plants need repotting, make sure their new pots either have drainage holes and a saucer to catch excess water or a thick layer of gravel in the bottom of the pot. But if all you want is a more attractive container, there is no need to repot. Use your imagination to come up with pretty or unusual plant containers that are big enough to hide the plastic pot and add zest to the décor of your room. If you use crocks or pottery bowls as containers, they will act as saucers for the plant. But if you put your potted plant in something that is not waterproof, like a pretty reed basket, be sure to put a saucer under the pot so the draining water won't damage the surface underneath.

Go wild! Almost anything can hold a potted plant. Besides

baskets and odd pieces of pottery, have you considered old metal potato chip tins? Or how about battered antique items like brass spittoons, chamber pots, wooden buckets, handle-less pitchers, or ice buckets? Perhaps you prefer the clean, simple lines of ordinary clay flower pots. Fill the bottom of a metal tray or old cookie sheet with gravel and assemble the pots on it for an indoor garden. (If you keep the gravel moist, the plants will thrive on the extra humidity!)

Is there an unused goldfish bowl or birdcage in your basement? Drag it out and show it off. It makes a super plant container. You can plant an open terrarium in a goldfish bowl. Put a layer of gravel and some planting charcoal in the bottom before adding soil. Use groupings of small plants; you can even add the little ceramic figures you had in the aquarium. A big spider plant looks super in a birdcage. The leaves are slender enough to grow through the bars and the little shoots will trail out. (Spider plants tend to produce more shoots if they are somewhat "pot-bound." You can use some of these shoots to add to the original plant or to start new ones.)

☆ slapdash tip

A Living Window Frame

If you have an ivy or other viny plant at the window, you can make an incredible living window frame. Just train the plant to go along both sides of the sill and up and around the window frame. You will need to tack or tape the vine to the window frame every foot (⅓ meter) or so as it grows to give it support. In time you will have a lovely green fringe all around your window!

A VINE FRAMING A WINDOW IS VERY PRETTY

Although large floor plants are rather expensive, they can provide dramatic focal points for your room. And there are some fairly large plants that you can easily grow from seed. An avocado pit suspended in water by three toothpicks stuck in its midsection will quickly grow roots. Then plant the rooted pit with the top half out of the soil and watch your baby avocado tree grow! Citrus fruit seeds planted in potting soil will quickly produce good-sized plants with shiny dark green leaves. (Try tearing off a little piece of leaf for a wonderful lemony smell!)

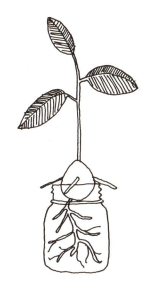

Since most of the decorating you do in your room is fairly permanent, you might enjoy a chance to experiment with different looks at a very small cost. Annual plants grown from vegetable seeds provide a great way to do this. You probably won't get any vegetables, but the plants themselves and their flowers are pretty and unusual. Try planting some seeds from the squash you had for dinner (let them dry for a few days first); in a few weeks you'll have beautiful leafy vines with big yellow trumpet-shaped flowers. Then next season, when these have died, try another vegetable such as beans, or some herbs that will spread their scent through your whole room. Basil, mint, parsley, and chives are all good.

THIS SQUASH BABY IS A FUTURE GREAT PLANT!

If you have fish or turtles or a bird in your room, you know how much pleasure

they can give. Why not make them a focal point of the room? Arrange chairs or cushions so you and your friends can easily see the fish flashing through the water; or hang the birdcage near your desk so you can watch your pet during study breaks. As with plants, just make sure that your pet's new environment makes it happy—direct sun and drafts should both be avoided. Remember, your pet's health is more important than your décor!

Green plants and other living things will add the finishing touches to the total look you've worked so hard to achieve. Now invite some friends over, sit back, and enjoy your great-looking new room!

Index

accessories, 44, 104–22
  battered antique, 120
  closet, 44
  desk-top, 111–13
  dresser, 115–16
  hamper as, 110–11
  lamps as, 104–08
  plants as, 118–21
  vanity-top, 113–15
  wastebaskets as, 108–10
aquarium, 34, 120

bag, drawstring, 45
bags, paper shopping, 45–46
basketball hoop plant hanger, 118–19
bedboard, 29
bed coverings, 71–83
bed, extra, 30–31
bed, fixing an uncomfortable, 29–30
bedspread, 71–75, 81–83
  making a, 74–75
  painted sheet, 73
  quilted, 81–83
  super easy, 72–73
  transforming an old, 71–72
belts, 44–45
bird, 121–22
birdcage, 120, 122
bookcase, board and cinder-block, 32–34
bookcase, stepped, 34
bottles, 53, 106–07
boxes, 115–16, 117–18
  cigar, 115–16
  hinged, 116
  see-through plastic, 117–18
box springs, 30, 78–81

bulletin board, 13, 14, 101–02
buttons, pin-on, 102

canopy, illusion bed, 94–96
cartons, 46–50
Celotex, 101
closet, organizing your, 43–46
closet rod, 43
closets and storage space, 43–51
collage, 13, 27, 35, 55, 106, 112, 115
color, 15–16
comforter, 75–77
contact paper, 13, 19, 24, 25–26, 29, 34–35, 49, 109
containers, 108, 110, 112–19
cubbyhole, 49
cupboard, corner, 50
cupcake tin, 117
curtains, 58–65, 68–69, 73
  café, 60–62
  "fake," 64–65
  full-length, 63
  shirred, 58–59, 60, 65, 68
  shower, 68–69
  used as door, 60
cushion, chair, 91

desk, 34–35
display, window, 53
display, ribbon, 102
drapes, 63
drapes, "fake," 64–65
drawer organizers, 117–18
drawers, painting, 20, 27, 35
dresser, vanity, 36–37, 73
dust ruffle, matching, 77–81

Easter basket, 113

fabric, 17, 19, 54, 56–57, 58–59, 61, 64, 71, 74, 78, 88–89, 93
fake fur, 87
fish, 121–22
floor plan, 13–15
floors, 85–91
flowerpots, 112, 119–20
foot locker, 50–51
frame, painted window, 55
framing pictures, 98–99
furniture, 13, 14–15, 23–41, 50–51
   arranging, 13–15, 23
   cardboard, 32
   fixing up old, 24–30, 50–51
   making your own, 31–41
   refinishing, 24–25
   secondhand, 23–24, 26
   unfinished, 31

garden, indoor, 120
glue and tape, 18
goldfish bowl, 120

hair ribbons, 44
hamper, 110–11
hangings, wall, 93–94
hardware, 18
headboard, wall, 103
hobby supplies, organizing, 13, 28, 46, 48
hooks, 46
hutch, 50

ivy, 120

jewelry, 44, 115–17

kitchen cabinet, 28–29
kitchen utensil tray, 117
knife, 18, 20
knobs, 26

lamp, making a, 106–08

lamps and lampshades, old, 104–07
look, the over-all, 15–17
loop, belt or necklace, 44–45

materials and tools, 17–20
mattress pad, foam, 29–30
measuring equipment, 18
measuring your room, 14–15
mirror, 38, 54, 115
mug rack, 44
Mylar, 54

nightstand, 50–51
night table, 40–41, 73

organizers, drawer, 117–18

paint, 19, 25
paint brush, 19
paint, fabric, 71–72, 73
painting, 19–20, 26–27
panels, side, 65
pegboard, 46
pets, 121–22
   environment for, 122
photo gallery, 98
pictures, framing, 98–99
pictures, hanging, 100
pillows, 17, 31, 50, 71, 88–91
pillows, floor, 88–90
plan, making a, 13–15
planting, 121
plants, 53, 118–22
   floor, 121
   hanging, 53, 118–19
   repotting, 119–20
   spider, 118, 120
   viny, 120
posters, 96–97
pots for plants, 119–20
prints and patterns, 16

remnants, fabric, 19

remnants, rug, 88
ribbon display, 102
rods, curtain, 58–59, 60–61, 63, 65–66, 95
room divider, 13, 47–48
rug, 85–88
    patchwork area, 87–88
    room-size, 85–86
    safari, 87

sand, colored, 106–08
scavenging, creative, 20–21
scissors and shears, 18
screen, folding, 13
sewing equipment, 18
shades, window, 55–57, 65
    decorating, 55, 56
    making your own, 56–57
sheets, uses for, 13, 17, 36, 41, 72–73, 76–83, 95–96, 106
shelves, window, 53, 118
shower curtain, decorative, 68–69
slipcover, 28
sports trophies, 53
spray painting, 20, 25, 29, 33, 73, 105
stain, wood, 25, 31
staple gun, 18
stencils, 56, 71–72, 73
stool, vanity, 38–40
storage chest/window seat, making a, 50–51
storage cubes, 43, 46–50
storage hutch, 50

storage unit, building a, 46–50
study area, 31

table, night, 40–41, 73
tape and glue, 18
tape, "pleater," 63
terrarium, 120
textures, 16–17
"throw," 27–28
tiebacks, 59, 65, 66–67
tools and materials, 17–20
trays, 114–15
turtles, 121–22

valances, 60, 62, 64, 65, 67–68
vanity dresser, 36–37, 73
vanity mirror, 38, 115
vanity stool, 38–40
varnish, 31, 35
velveteen, 116
view, 56

wall hangings, 93–94
wallpaper, leftover, 110
"wallpaper," do-it-yourself, 97–98
walls, 93–103
wastebaskets, 68, 108–10
window display, 53
window, framed, 54–55
window, mirrored, 54
window seat/storage chest, making a, 50–51
windows, 53–68, 120
wood, 32

ABOUT THE AUTHORS

Carol Barkin received her B.A. from Radcliffe College, where she majored in English. She and her husband have traveled widely in Europe, the Far East, and the United States, and became friends with Elizabeth James when they lived for a time on the West Coast. In addition to editing and writing for a children's periodical, Ms. Barkin has had several years' experience editing adult and children's books in the United States and in London. She and her husband now live in New York City, with their newborn son.

Elizabeth James (Mrs. David Marks) received her B.A. in mathematics from Colorado College, where she minored in experimental psychology, and continued her studies at UCLA and California State College at Long Beach. A consultant in educational television, she has written scripts for both theatrical and documentary films as well as educational television programs. She and her husband live in Beverly Hills, California.